IN DEFENCE OF THE REALM

First published in 2003 by

WOODFIELD PUBLISHING
Bognor Regis, West Sussex, England
www.woodfieldpublishing.com

ISBN 1-903953-35-9

In Defence of the Realm

*An 'Erk'-some account of National
Service in the Royal Air Force 1954-56*

PETER VOYSE

Woodfield

To my late brothers Alfred and Kenneth
who also served.

Contents

Foreword

From the end of the Second World War, up and till the end of 1960 over two and a quarter of a million young men were called up, on what was known as 'National Service'. They had to leave home, often travelling away from their families, for the first time in their lives, and spend two years in the service of their sovereign and country.

Some looked upon it with severe trepidation, whilst others, who had perhaps been in the cadet forces, the Boy Scouts, the Boy's Brigade, or other similar youth organisations, took to service life with no worries whatsoever.

The British Empire was still fairly large and National Servicemen were likely to be posted to the Four Corners of the globe. There were conflicts in many parts of the world as colonies under the rule of Great Britain struggled to achieve their independence. Britain's youth found themselves embroiled in affairs they understood very little about and sadly many gave their lives in distant lands, never completing their National Service. Young men who had hardly ever travelled further than the seaside in their own country, prior to National Service, found themselves policing difficult situations in foreign countries. They were often abused in languages they didn't understand and were hated just because they wore the uniform of the country, which had rule over the everyday lives of people whose country they occupied.

Some of the conflicts were serious and National Servicemen fought and died in major wars such as the Korean War, fighting under the flag of the United Nations and under the control of generals from other countries. They found themselves trekking through jungles and being eaten alive by all sorts of nasty insects, contracting tropical diseases such as malaria.

Nearly every National Serviceman will have a tale to tell ranging from the sad, to the extremely funny. The majority of them went into the services with an innocent naivety and came out as mature young men, well disciplined and a credit to the various services in which they had served. Most, if they are honest with themselves, benefited from the strict life and learned to cope with most things that perhaps modern youth would balk at and protest.

Most went in at eighteen years of age, but there were others who were older. Some had been granted a deferment whilst they completed an apprenticeship, whilst others completed a spell at university before having to 'do their stint'. There was no way of avoiding the 'call up', unless you failed the medical examination. Some people refused to go and served prison sentences for their beliefs. In many parts of the country, it was common to see the words, 'CUT THE CALL UP' written on the side of bridges or on large areas of blank wall. Regardless of the protest National Service continued for many years.

Some people are of the opinion that National Service should have continued, it certainly would not harm some individuals to go through what the youth of those days experienced.

Contained in this book are the experiences of one National Serviceman, not a hero by any means, but someone who left home and served his time. It is hoped that readers will get an understanding of the period and the trials, tribulations and often funny experiences of the author and his pals in uniform.

Peter Voyse, 2003

The author (centre, holding certificate), still in uniform some 40 years after the events described in this book, retires from the special Constabulary after 12 years service with the South Yorkshire police.

In RAF uniform 1954.

About the Author

Peter Voyse lives with his wife Elsie in the suburb of Frecheville in the City of Sheffield. After leaving the R.A.F. he went back to the grocery and provisions trade for one year. In 1957 he joined the Sheffield Transport Department as a Bus Conductor and stayed with the firm nearly thirty years, retiring from the successor company, the South Yorkshire Passenger Transport Executive in the rank of Chief Traffic Officer in 1986. During his years 'on the buses' Peter was successively, Bus Conductor, Bus Driver, Traffic Regulator, Traffic Inspector, Instructor Inspector, Senior Investigations Officer and Chief Traffic Officer.

Twelve years service with the South Yorkshire Police Special Constabulary saw Peter receive a long service and good conduct medal. He retired from that service in the rank of Section Officer.

In 1958 Peter married Elsie and they have three children - a son and two daughters. They have two grandsons and four granddaughters with an additional grandchild due in November 2003.

The author continues to work three days per week as the Personnel Manager with Leger Holidays one of the largest coach tour operators in the United Kingdom.

Preface

In the early 1960s, as a young Bus Driver, I used to sit fascinated in mobile canteen buses, mess rooms and canteens and listen to the stories of ex-servicemen, who were my working colleagues. The Second World War had only been over less than twenty years and the memories of their experiences were still fresh in the minds of these men who were in their thirties and forties.

In 1968, I joined an organisation named 'The Fellowship of the Services', an ex-servicemen's association dedicated to the welfare of former servicemen of all the three services. Again I was able to listen to the tales of those who had served, both King George the VI and his daughter Queen Elizabeth II.

I always thought it a pity that these men very rarely wrote down their war and peacetime experiences. Some of the stories were tragic, some of the men suffered real hardships, but many of the stories I found were very funny.

A work colleague, who had served through the war in the RAF, relayed one typical story to me. Walter, who sadly died in early 2000, told me of a time when he was stationed at RAF Little Snoring. At that time it was the practice to disperse aircraft at what were known as 'satellite' dromes. At each of the sites, two or three aircraft would be parked on hard standings and around the area would be a number of Nissen huts in which the ground crews for the aircraft would be accommodated. Walter told me that, in their particular hut, there was an airman whose trade was MT (Motor Transport) driver. This man never mixed with the rest of the lads and in Walter's words 'was a right misery'. All the lads were issued with bicycles, to enable them to cycle up to the main camp for cookhouse and some of the other facilities, which were not available at the satellite sites. Walt said that, in the summer it was quite pleasant cycling along the perimeter track of an evening, but on wet and windy nights, it was miserable. It mattered not how bad the weather was, the miserable MT driver, never offered anyone a lift in his lorry. Walter said that all the lads got together and discussed how they could get at the unsociable airman. What they decided to do was this, one winter's morning, they all arose from their beds at around 3 o'clock. They all walked about the Nissen hut, making a lot of noise and wearing towels around their necks, as though they were going to or from the ablutions. Eventually, the MT man woke up, shook his watch and quickly got out of bed. He went and washed, went out without speaking to anyone, started his lorry up and drove off into the darkness. All the other lads went back to bed, satisfied that their trick had worked and they had got their own back on the unsociable and uncharitable airman. Unfortunately however, they never got any satisfaction from the episode, said Walter. This was because the man never spoke to anyone, he never said anything about the episode the next time they saw him.

Well Walter never got to write his story down, but I decided to start writing down my short service life with the RAF. I got the 'Introduction' and 'Chapter One' done and then seemed to lose interest, my typed copy lying in the cupboard for a long time. In early 1999, I was encouraged by Ted Caton, another ex-'erk' to complete my book. Ted had written a book himself and, with his encouragement, I started to write my story. Ted very kindly 'proof-read' each completed chapter and helped me on my way.

It is thanks to Ted and my wife's patience that I finally finished my story. I have managed to tell my tale and also pass on a funny story of another 'erk', who could probably have told many more stories, if he had been given the same encouragement as I received.

Finally, the writing of the book has been long and arduous, not having my own computer I have had to use that of my daughter Jane and son-in-law David, to whom I am thankful. Each Friday night for many months, whilst on 'baby-sitting' duties, I have left my wife with the grandchildren and the television and repaired to my daughter's bedroom to do my bit of typing. Being the end of the week and the end of a long day, I have inevitably made some mistakes, both in spelling and grammar. Thankfully Ted Caton has filtered out many of the errors, but I am aware of a number of mistakes and hope that the reader will forgive my carelessness.

Glossary

AC2	Aircraftman 2nd Class
AC1	Aircraftman 1st Class
LAC	Leading Aircraftman
SAC	Senior Aircraftman
CPL	Corporal
SGT	Sergeant
F/SGT	Flight Sergeant
Chiefie	Flight Sergeant
FLT/LT	Flight Lieutenant

Introduction

The snow flurried down on to an already white land. The yellow grey sky gave a promise of more to come. The Lancashire countryside looked like a Christmas card, with the exception of a large rectangular-shaped mound that protruded from the ground, like some ancient burial site. On a levelled out piece of ground at the side of the mound stood a number of parked vehicles, three lorries, their canvas backs sagging under the weight of snow, and three utility looking coaches. Just in front of one of the lorries stood a signboard on posts, the board bore the words '*Royal Air Force Police Dogs Patrol This Area*'.

This was the site of one of a chain of underground operation centres used in the defence of Great Britain, and part of the system, which along with other operation centres, scattered around Europe, formed the 'eyes and ears' of the N.A.T.O. air forces.

Inside the 'block' (as it was known, by the airmen who worked there), it was warm if not cosy. Sixty feet under the ground in a brightly lit Operations room, bored looking airmen sat around a gigantic map of the United Kingdom, Ireland and the coastal regions of Western Europe. Each man was wearing a headset with earphones and with a speaking tube resting on his chest, the type of old-fashioned equipment that telephone operators used to wear. The map was clear of the plotting equipment that usually covered it, representing aircraft flying over the British Isles. The wintry weather outside had put a stop to all thoughts of flying for that day. Nevertheless the radar stations around the country continued to search the skies, regardless of the weather, even though no information was forthcoming. Only a fool would be out flying today.

High above the 'Ops' room was a cabin with sloping glass leaning out over the room at an angle, this was the Control Officer's room. At a long bench littered with telephones, switches and various piles of paper there sat a young officer.

Pilot Officer Cotton held a telephone to his ear and, looking seriously at a piece of paper in front of him said, 'Baker four', at the same time he made a mark with his pen on the paper. From the other end of the telephone came the reply, 'Negative'. Down on the floor of the Operations room, the Duty Corporal turned to one of the 'erks' (airmen), who was sitting at the bottom end of the plotting map and said, 'I wonder what old Cotton is up to, he's been on the phone for ages?'.

Just at that point the relief crew came in for their one hour stint in the 'Ops' room. The plotters took down headsets from the racks on the wall situated near to the entrance of the 'Ops' room, each airman slung the mouthpieces round their necks and fastened them. One by one they then plugged into the positions around the large map. The airmen being relieved unplugged their sets and handed over their plotting rods to the take-over men. As the new Duty Corporal came in, he was made aware of the present position nation-wide. His mate then said, 'I'm nipping up to the 'Ops' cabin to see what old Cotton's up to, there's no flying and yet he's been on to R.A.F. Valley for ages, when I switched into the line in the P.B.X. (switchboard), all I could hear was, 'Able Two' and the person at the other end of the line saying 'Negative".

The now off duty corporal made his way out of the 'Ops' room, up the back staircase and along the upper corridor, with its side view over the 'Ops' room, and then on into the control cabin. Making it look as though he was there on official business, he stood looking at the weather map on the wall of the room. The map showed the weather state of every airfield in the United Kingdom. The corporal moved round slowly until he was looking over the shoulder of Pilot Officer Cotton. To his amazement the officer was playing the game 'Battleships and Cruisers', a game in which two players mark off a graph with the letters 'A' to 'H' down the side and the numbers '1' to '8' along the top. The players then mark the squares in the graph with letters, representing Battleship (B), Cruiser (C), Submarine (S), etc. Pilot Officer Cotton was using the direct telephone lines through to R.A.F. Valley and the man on the other end would be the Duty Air Traffic Controller.

The corporal hurriedly returned to the 'Ops' room, made his mate aware of what was happening and then suggested they play a prank on Cotton. They plugged the P.B.X. line into a wire recorder, (the forerunner of the tape recorder), and for the next quarter of an hour recorded every move in Pilot Officer Cotton's game. Later that day, when Cotton had put down the phone and had picked up a book, he was alerted by the tinkling of one of the telephones in front of him. Picking up the phone he said, 'Operations control', he was greeted by a recording of his own voice saying, 'Charlie five'; he took it all in good part.

One wonders what the Russians would have thought if they had intercepted any of the original conversations between the two R.A.F. officers.

The story is true, I know, I was on duty in the 'Ops' room at the time. I was part of the defence force looking after the citizens of the United Kingdom, who would no doubt have gone to their beds in the safe knowledge that their air force was second to none.

1. Called Up

(In which I receive a call from the Queen)

'Peter...!' It was the third time that my mother had called me. I knew that if I lingered in bed any longer, the tone of her voice would change and the request for me to get up would be replaced by an order, with threats attached like, 'If you don't get up now...', followed by what I could expect if I didn't move myself. A few seconds more of my warm bed and then I plucked up courage to place my warm foot on to the cold linoleum floor covering. Shivering, I pulled on my clothes and made my way downstairs. I had two flights of stairs to go down and the smell of toast hurried me on my way to the cellar kitchen.

As I started down the stone steps which led to the kitchen, the sound of the letter box flap made me turn in my tracks. I saw that a couple of letters had arrived in today's post and were lying on the hall floor. I went back and picked up the two envelopes. One was marked 'Littlewood's Pools' and contained a dream of luxury, and the other was a brown envelope on which was printed in bold type, **O.H.M.S.**, (On Her Majesty's Service). This envelope was addressed to me. With mixed feelings I slid my finger along the inside of the top of the envelope, ripping it open in an untidy manner. Inside was a buff piece of paper, which was neatly folded. I opened up the paper feverishly; it carried instructions for me to report for a medical to qualify whether or not I was fit to serve my Queen and Country. I went downstairs and showed the letter to my Mum, if I was proved to be medically fit, I would be the third of her sons to serve in the armed forces. My eldest brother had been with the Royal Ordinance Corps., after serving his two years he had just been demobbed. Most of his service had been spent in Kenya where the 'Mau Mau' terrorist troubles had started. As the problems had erupted just prior to his departure from that country, we used to kid him on, by saying that he had caused trouble. My other elder brother, who is two years my senior, was serving his time with the Royal Signal Corps., he was stationed in Germany. In a letter to me he had said that, when I went for my medical and was interviewed, I should ask for a 'compassionate' posting into the 'Signals', so that I could be with him.

When I went to work that day, the talk all day was mainly about my forthcoming medical. Some of my work-mates had served in the war and were full of 'old sweats' stories. I was told what to expect when I went for my medical, how I would have to drop my trousers and 'cough' and that sometimes it was a lady doctor. The next few weeks were a mixture of excitement and trepidation, I half wanted to pass my medical with flying colours and be sure that nothing was wrong with me, and half wanted to fail so that I would not have to face having to leave home. I started thinking up illnesses which were serious enough to disqualify me from military service, whilst were not serious enough to endanger my future. Perhaps I might go deaf, or maybe there was a possibility my eyes would be defective in some way, or maybe I had some mysterious disease which wasn't apparent to the normal view, but would be diagnosed by the team of doctors. In any way, it would not be long before I would find out.

On the eve of my medical, out came the tin bath at home. It was filled from the gas geyser, which was over the sink in our kitchen. We thought we were 'posh' because we had an instant supply of hot water at hand. We had an ingenious method of filling the bath, by using the metal extension pipes of the vacuum cleaner. The chrome pipe was jammed over the spot of the geyser at one end, whilst the other end rested over the galvanised bath. Bath time at our house was not for the modest, the only protection you had from view from the others was the clothes horse draped with a bed sheet and opened around the side of the bath. Skilful manoeuvring of the towel was developed and it was necessary for you to get out of the bath with your back to everyone. The first one to take a bath was the lucky one, he got the clean water; others had to make do by adding further hot water to the predecessors' left over water. Emptying the water was a work of art and required great teamwork, the bath being slid slowly but surely, in small jerks, across the kitchen floor to the door. Too much of a jerk would sometimes set off an uncontrollable wave motion slopping water over the end of the bath soaking the pegged rug. On successfully reaching the kitchen door the bath would be up-tipped by lifting it with the handle fitted on the end. In what was sometimes an 'Herculean' effort the water was poured out of the kitchen door and into the backyard, some water going down the grate in the middle of the yard and some overflowing onto the garden, where it slowly soaked away.

The day of my medical dawned bright and clear, I was full of nervous apprehension. I got up, had my breakfast, washed the bed out of my eyes and off I went. Catching the tram at the bottom of our road, I paid my fare to Ecclesall Road bottom, where I then had to transfer on to another vehicle bound for Ecclesall, I had previously ascertained the whereabouts of the Medical Centre and alighted at Hickmott Road. With a frightened feeling of the unknown, which made my heart pound in my chest, I made my way into the medical centre where I reported to a clerk who was seated at a desk. I handed over the papers I had received in the post and was told to take a seat. For a short time I was engaged in a nervous conversation with one of the other youths who was also waiting for a medical. After a period of about 15 minutes we were led into a large room, which was partitioned off into small cubicles. We were instructed to strip off to just our trousers. Then it was a case of moving from cubicle to cubicle, in each one a different test was carried out. Eyes were tested, ears were looked into, lights were shone down the throat and so on.

Finally the order came to 'drop your trousers', and then there was the acute embarrassment of a complete stranger, albeit a doctor, grasping your testicles and giving the command to, 'cough!' After the medical came a short aptitude test, which I found very interesting. I felt I had done well in the test. Finally, I was interviewed and asked which branch of the armed forces I had a preference for. In my mind I thought, 'none of them', I was worried about going away from home. In reality, I said, 'Well my brother is in the Royal Signals, so I wouldn't mind going in that regiment, especially if I could get with him in Germany'. Little did I know how bureaucracy works, ask for what you want and you will get something completely different. Tell them what you don't want and there is every chance that you will come up trumps.

The short interview finished with the words; 'you will be contacted by post!' Off I went into the world of normal people to commence another period of waiting. And so I spent the summer of 1954 waiting to serve my country. The occasional letter from my brother Ken, in Germany, bucked me up by telling me of the good things about service life. The daily news reports of the happenings in Cyprus and Egypt made me have sleepless nights. My friend, Tony Baxter, wrote to me from Malaya, a country torn by strife, with terrorist attacks happening every other day.

The summer went by and slowly turned into autumn, I was feeling a little blasé about things, maybe with the thousands of documents being processed, mine had somehow been mislaid, perhaps they had forgotten me in some way. I went to the cinema on almost a nightly basis, my constant companion was my friend Mick Dickinson. We were some of the last out of our group of local lads who were still civilians; most of our mates were now in the forces.

In the middle of August came the dreaded call, in the form of another buff coloured envelope, the letter inside instructed me to report to, 'Royal Air Force, Cardington', in the county of Bedfordshire. Also enclosed in the envelope was a travel warrant, which was to exchange for a single railway ticket from Sheffield to Bedford. The letter also instructed me what to take in the way of personal possessions. Included in the list was a 'gummed label', I could not think what that was for; but it would not be too long before I found out. My joining date became another birthday; that is, I would remember it all my life, the 6th of September 1954.

The next few weeks gave me an idea of what a condemned man must feel like, I counted off the days. Each day at work I was reminded of my impending 'doom'; older men gave me advice, younger lads looked up to me, whilst the girls, promised to 'write'. Eventually came my final day at work. I drew all the money I was entitled to and my mates had a collection for me. One of the sons of the family business I was employed by, gave me a whole one pound note, shook my hand and wished me, 'good luck'.

On the Saturday, I went round my friends and relations and then spent my last night at the cinema, with my friend Mick, who was shortly to follow me into the R.A.F. On the Sunday night before I went away from home, to serve my Queen and country, I was so nervous that I got into the bath with my watch on, ruining a good watch. My night was slept in fits of tossing and turning, with thoughts of Cyprus, Malaya, East Africa and Egypt. Which of these places filled with trouble and strife would I be sent to? Would I finish up in any of them?

Tomorrow the great adventure was to start...

2. RAF Cardington

(in which I become a 'sprog')

Grasping my poor quality suitcase and with my gabardine mac over my arm, I said goodbye to my mother at the garden gate, outside our large Victorian house in Sheffield. Mum was in her everyday housewife dress of flowered coverall and a turban on her head, a legacy of the Second World War, when she had worked on munitions in a factory. Loose flowing hair was frowned upon in those factory conditions, when working with machinery.

As I walked along the road, I kept turning around waving to my mother, until I went over the brow of the hill and she disappeared from sight, This was the start of a great adventure. In the 1950's young people didn't travel far from home. The furthest I had travelled was in 1953, when, during the week of the Queen's coronation, accompanied by my two friends, I had cycled to Newmarket in Suffolk, to see my brother Alfred. Prior to that it had been trips to the seaside, Skegness, Cleethorpes, and Blackpool, being three of the places I had visited, I certainly had not done much travelling by train and never by myself.

It was a lovely morning, as I reached and crossed the main A61 road. The road to the left led to Chesterfield, whilst I would be travelling to the right towards central Sheffield. The city had one of the best tramway systems in the country and I joined a queue at the tram-stop, feeling a bit worried about what was in front of me. Other people in the queue were probably heading for their places of work, which was possibly no different from what they had done last week and what they would be doing for the following week, and the rest of the year. I was at the start of a special journey, a journey that would take me to a life where I had no control over my own destiny, for two full years.

The tramcar came along and I boarded and paid my fare to town. The tram was on a journey to the other side of the town and its destination blinds read, 'Wadsley Bridge via Shoreham Street'. I sat upstairs as it rocked its way into Sheffield, passing the Sheffield United football ground on the left and later the Sheffield Transport tram-shed on the right, at the very end of Shoreham Street. I alighted at the next stop, which on the fare – table was known as 'Stage 2 – Midland Station'. The tram-stop was situated on the traffic island in the middle of the road. It was a downhill walk to the station, the main structure of which has remained the same since it was built in the nineteenth century; a series of arches with pointed roofs over each arch.

I walked down to the station, where I exchanged my travel warrant for a 'one way' ticket to the town of Bedford, in Bedfordshire. Presenting my ticket to the ticket inspector at the entrance to the station, I was directed to the correct platform where the maroon coloured train was standing with a 'Jubilee' class steam engine at its head. The engine was simmering away gently, ready for its part in taking me away from my home-town. I boarded the train and made my way along the corridor to a compartment and awaited the train's departure.

A shrill blast of the whistle and a waving of the guard's green flag, signalled the train's exodus from the Sheffield Midland station. For the first few miles the train travelled along the Sheaf Valley, in a southerly direction, which valley I had just travelled, in the opposite direction by tramcar. From the train window, I could see places that I recognized, including the road I had so recently walked down, from my home. I was all ready feeling the first pangs of home-sickness. The steam engine worked hard on the up-gradient out of Sheffield, with Millhouses Park appearing on the right hand side of the track. Shortly we passed through the last station in Yorkshire, Dore & Totley, and then on into the Bradway tunnel. The train burst out into Derbyshire, through Dronfield and Unstone, and on into Chesterfield, where a stop was made. From the station there was a marvellous view of the famous crooked spire.

Once the train left Chesterfield, I was in unfamiliar territory. We travelled southward through Derby, where I was interested in the variety of railway engines and rolling stock in the area of the station. The journey to Bedford was uneventful and I spent most of the time looking out of the carriage window, and eating the sandwiches packed by my mother.

The arrival at Bedford found me a bit panicky. I took my case and coat down from the luggage rack and made my way out of the train, and on to the platform of the station. I looked for the 'way out' sign and made my way along the platform. Nearby the station exit was a small shed-like office, which I later found was an R.T.O. (Rail Transport Office), the domain of a member of the services, whose job it was to help direct travelling servicemen. Such offices were to be found on most major railway stations.

An R.A.F. policeman was standing by the R.T.O. in all his glory; white topped cap, white webbing belt, shoulder strap and white gaiters. His boots gleamed against the dark platform surface and the creases in his trousers looked as sharp as knives. The two stripes on his arms stood out well against the blue material of his uniform and on his left arm he wore an armband of red and black banding, with the letters, R.A.F.P. being prominently displayed.

I suddenly became aware that there were other young men carrying small suitcases, all heading towards the station exit. The R.A.F. policeman stood forward, and in the form of a question said, 'R.A.F. Cardington?' I was one of those that nodded, wondering innocently how he knew who I was out of the stream of people leaving the station. On reflection, we must have stood out like a sore thumb. We were directed towards a small utility Bedford coach, in R.A.F. blue, which was parked on the station approach. I boarded the coach, where I joined a number of other young men, who had already chosen a seat on the coach. I sat down on one of the slatted wooden seats, nodding at the lad sitting in the seat immediately behind. Little did I realize that some of the people I was travelling with on the coach would be my constant companions for the next nine weeks. One lad on the coach I would be with for the full two years of my R.A.F. service.

After a few minutes, the driver climbed into the driving seat. He was dressed in blue battledress (working blue) and wearing a beret, and, as far as smartness was concerned, at the opposite end of the spectrum from the R.A.F. policeman I had just seen. The engine was started and the coach moved off into the town of Bedford. I looked out of the coach window, people were shopping and going about their everyday business, no one gave a second look at the R.A.F. vehicle as it moved through the town. We crossed over the bridge, which spanned the River Ouse, and on out of the county town of Bedfordshire, east, towards the village of Cardington.

I wasn't aware at the time how famous was the R.A.F. station to which I was being taken. It was from R.A.F. Cardington that the infamous air-ship R101, set out on the 4th of October 1930, on a flight to India. Amongst the passengers on that fateful flight was the British Air Minister of that time, Christopher Birchwood Thompson, (Lord Thompson of Cardington). Along with 48 other persons, including members of the airship's crew, the Air Minister was destined to perish in the early hours of the morning of 5th October 1930, when the airship crashed into a hillside near

Beauvais in France. Most of the victims are buried in a mass grave in the cemetery opposite St. Mary's church, Cardington, where a memorial to those who died can be seen. In the church are artefacts recovered from the wreckage, including the burned Royal Air Force ensign that flew from the R101's tail. I was not to see the church, the artefacts or the memorial until the 1990s, so I return to my story and the 1950s.

The coach travelled through the countryside, the engine whining in the way peculiar to all Bedford commercial vehicles. I was to get very used to that sound, from both coaches and high-wheeled base lorries, such as the Bedford 'Garry', and the newer vehicles, which were replacing that marque in the British armed services. Eventually, we came to the perimeter fence of R.A.F. Cardington and ran along-side this until we came to the camp entrance. The coach pulled into the entrance and came to a stop opposite the camp guardroom, outside which stood a couple of RAF service policemen (SPs), one holding a clipboard.

The coach driver invited us to get off the coach. Once off the coach we were told to line up in threes as our name was called out. My name was eventually called out and I joined the rest of those lined up. We all stood there untidily grasping our suitcases, most of us had a gabardine mac on or slung over our arm, (they were the height of fashion at that time). The SPs marched, or more accurately, walked us down the camp roads to a series of wooden huts, taking us into the door of one. The door led into a short corridor at the end of the hut and we filed in one by one. My allocated bed was the first on the right, just inside the hut and was simply an iron frame with three 'biscuit' mattresses piled on top of each other at the head of the bed. An airman, dressed in 'working blue', had been awaiting our arrival and he told us to leave our possessions on our beds and follow him. I had not seen the SPs leave, but we were now obviously in the charge of a lowly 'erk' (airman). He took us to a bedding store where we were issued with 2 sheets, 2 pillows and pillowcases, and five blankets. We were taken back to the hut where we were shown by our guardian 'erk', how to make up our bed and how to make 'hospital corners' with the sheets and blankets. After the demonstration was over the airman took us to the cookhouse, where we had our first taste of R.A.F. food. On the way, the airman showed us the N.A.A.F.I. (Navy, Army and Air Force Institution) where he said we could get some proper food if we wished, later in the day.

Whilst having the meal, I 'palled up' with a friendly young man who hailed from Cambridge, his name was Ted. I was able to carry on a conversation with him, as I had passed through the suburbs of Cambridge the previous year, on a visit to my brother in Newmarket, so I felt we had something in common. Also at the table was another young man who I was destined to get to know very well. Chris was from Dewsbury, in Yorkshire, and had, unknowing to me at the time, travelled on the same train as me from Yorkshire to Bedfordshire. Chris was to stay with me throughout my service and we both left the R.A.F. on the same day.

We eventually returned to the hut, where our guardian airman outlined what would be happening over the next few days. He advised us to write home, but said that we would not be able to give an address, as we would not be at Cardington long enough to receive mail. He then showed us where the ablutions were so that we could have a wash and brush up. After a further short talk the airman left, saying that the rest of the day was ours, and that he would, 'see us the next morning'. I wrote a letter home and then joined some of the others on a visit to the N.A.A.F.I.. Whilst there I bought a silk handkerchief, emblazoned with the Royal Air Force crest, as a present for my sixteen year old sister, whose birthday was imminent on the 26th of September. After about two hours of exchanging stories, we made our way back to the hut. It was strange for me to undress in front of complete strangers, but I eventually donned my 'civvie' pyjamas and climbed into bed. At exactly 11 o'clock, or as we came to call it 2300hours, the hut lights went out. It was time to try to get some sleep. Someone in the hut was sobbing and I must admit I was feeling homesick. Eventually I fell asleep, my first day in the R.A.F. complete. According to my calculations, I had another 729 days to go.

The next few days were a round of mental and physical tests; we had our eyes looked in to, our hearing tested by someone whispering from the other side of the room. We were checked to see whether we were free from infection' (FFI), another case of dropping your trousers. We were given a Morse code test and did a further aptitude test. In between these activities, we were kitted out with our various pieces of equipment; knives, forks and spoons were issued and stamped with our individual service numbers. I had been allocated my service number and would remember it for the rest of my life, like every other serviceman. I was now 2733153 Aircraftsman Second Class Voyse.

On our visit to the clothing stores I was surprised that we were measured for our 'best blue', officially known as 'No. 1 dress'. Having seen films where recruits had clothing thrown at them, the last thing I expected was a tailor making chalk marks on the jacket and trousers of the walking out uniform. The 'Number 2 dress', or battle-dress was a blouson jacket and although not tailored, it fitted me very well. We started wearing this uniform almost immediately, civilian clothes being packed away in our suitcase. Great trouble was experienced with the shirt collars issued. We had been advised to bring a set of collar studs with us and the fitting of these into the collar-less shirts was no problem, neither was there any bother in attaching the collars to the shirts. It was when we tried to bend the collars from the upright position. It was a two-man job and a knee in the back for the first few minutes, it was a nightmare putting on a fresh collar. I had never had so many clothes, there was a great-coat, which fitted well and was very warm, gloves, three pair of socks, shirts, vests and underpants, (or as they were shown on the clothing list, 'drawers —cellular- airman'), pullover, tie, and braces.

The beret was another item, which was somewhat uncontrollable, one of the signs of a 'sprog' was the flying beret. A long serving airman would have a beret, which flopped down on one side, with the cap badge showing proud to the front. A new beret stood out at the side and looked like a flying saucer. We were also issued with an amount of service webbing, belts, straps, and also a large backpack and small pack, ammunition pouches, a bayonet scabbard and water bottle. A large white kit bag was issued with a blue band around it and with 'R.A.F.' and 2733153 VOYSE, stamped on the canvas.

When we eventually received our 'best-blue', we were photographed outside the hut, resplendent in our peaked caps and looking very smart. I must admit that I felt very good in the uniform and was proud to wear it.

On one of the days at Cardington, we were taken into a hut that had a series of pew-like fitments. We all stood behind the pews holding a block in front of us with our service number displayed. There was a photographer with a camera on a tripod and he took photos of six of us at a time, two tiers of three. The photo was for our identity card, R.A.F. form 1250, which we called our 'twelve-fifty'. Another day we were transported down to some huts which were quite close to the massive hangars, (which can still be seen at Cardington today), and as were described previously, these were the storage sheds for the air-ships

R100 and R101. We were surprised to see an Austin lorry emerge from one of the hangars, with a large barrage balloon floating above the lorry and attached to it by a cable. Underneath the balloon was a square box-like structure. When the lorry was well clear of the hangar, the balloon started to rise until it was well above the hangars and appeared small in the sky. Suddenly we saw objects fall from the box-like structure and parachutes break open, we were watching a training session of soldiers from the Parachute Regiment, the famous 'Red Berets'. These were their initial jumps prior to doing drops from a moving aircraft.

We were told to parcel up our cases, full of our 'civvie' attire, and fasten on a label with our home address. These were then collected from us and sent home. It was quite traumatic, cutting our last link with home. Again I for one suffered some homesickness pangs, as I imagined my Mum receiving my stuff at home.

The time spent at Cardington was a gentle breaking-in period and in no way prepared us for what was to come.

Just before I move on, there were two incidents, which occurred at Cardington, that stick in my mind. Our guardian airman advised us of a weekly dance at the camp, when girls were bussed in from the surrounding districts. A gang of us went up to the place where the dance was being held, resplendent in our new uniforms. Ted and I stood like wallflowers at the side of the dance-floor watching the dancing. Unfortunately there was a fight which developed between some airmen and some lads in civilian clothing, which ended in the R.A.F. police dragging the brawling airmen out of the hall. Ted and I made our way out of the dance, I had never seen a proper fight before. I still remember the tune that was being played at the time of the incident; it was, 'Walking my baby back home'. I don't know what happened to the civilian lads, or how they came to be at the dance, they were more than likely ejected from the camp. I can well imagine that the fighting 'erks' probably spent the next week on 'jankers' (punishment detail).

The other incident involved a young lad, (who I will call Brian). Brian looked like a schoolboy. We all looked young, but Brian had the face of a very young boy and he could have passed for a twelve or thirteen year old. He was a lively character and full of the joy of life. One night we were all settling down in our beds after 'lights out', when suddenly the hut door opened and in rushed Brian. Although we couldn't see him, we could identify him from the sound of his voice. He was very excited and to all and sundry shouted, " I've just s......d that blonde bird from the N.A.A.F.I.", crudely letting us all know that he had had sexual relations with the young lady, who we had all mentally noted, on our visits to the N.A.A.F.I.. Everyone told Brian to shut up and get to bed, and to stop imagining things. Everyone was convinced that he was hallucinating; events later were to prove us wrong.

And so our initial period of service came to a close. The first days had been quite easy; in a few days we had been transformed into what looked like airmen. At least we were all dressed alike and there was something of a bonding developing between us. The eighteen in our hut had kept together, whilst we were aware of another 70 'sprogs', from other huts, whose paths we had crossed during the activities of those first few days in the service.

Our guardian airman informed us that the intake to which we belonged, was destined to go to R.A.F. West Kirby, which we were told was on the Larton Wirral. For all that I knew of the geography of the country, it might as well have been Timbuktu. The discussions amongst us, on that last evening in the NA.A.F.I. at Cardington, were mainly rumours about West Kirby. Some said it was the worst square-bashing posting, whilst others said that they had heard that Padgate, Bridgenorth, Wilmslow or Hednesford (all square-bashing establishments), were far worse. We would soon find out.

3. RAF West Kirby

(in which I become a 'trained killer')

The majority of those who joined on the same day as me travelled to R.A.F. West Kirby. We were aware of a number who had been selected for officer training. At least two from our hut had been posted elsewhere. In total about 80 to a hundred 'sprog' airmen, fully kitted, joined the special train which was to take us direct to West Kirby. In those pre-Dr. Beeching days, there were branch lines all over the country and even the remotest towns and villages had their own railway station or halt. R.A.F. Cardington had its own 'spur' of track, and it was from the camp itself that we commenced our journey.

We were all issued with a packed lunch, which we placed in our small pack. Laden down with all of our equipment, (large webbing pack on the back, water bottle and bayonet scabbard at the sides of our webbing belt, and shoulder straps fitted at the front with ammunition pouches, and last but not least, our kit bag containing our No.1 dress, cap, etc.), we boarded the train. I have no idea which route the train took, but it seemed an age before we arrived at the tiny station that served West Kirby. The resort of West Kirby stands by the River Dee estuary and adjoins Hoylake, on the Wirral peninsula. We were destined to see little of the area, other than the countryside immediately surrounding the camp.

Standing in the station yard were a number of R.A.F. lorries, with canvas backs. We were told to put our kit bags in one of the lorries and to board one of the other lorries, which we did. Still being lumbered with our webbing and back packs, it was a difficult manoeuvre. Eventually, when all the trucks were loaded, we moved off on the short journey to the camp. The lorries travelled in convoy through the country lanes, carrying their cargo of subdued 'sprog' airmen.

The lorries finally turned into the camp gates, where two sentries stood outside their sentry boxes. The camp guardroom appeared on the right hand side and the lorries turned right and on to the camp road system. The lorries stopped on the large parade ground, parking in a semi-circle. We became aware of raised voices and got our first glimpse of the drill instructors, who we would get to know very well over the next eight weeks. They were bawling their heads off and as the drivers of the lorries dropped the backs down, we were told in no uncertain terms, to 'get yourselves down here' and 'move yourselves'. We needed no second telling and with pounding hearts and fearful looks on our faces, we descended on to a patch of ground which we would come to hate.

"Get fell in to threes", we were instructed. Whilst we were scrambling into lines of three, the drivers were throwing our lovely new kit bags on to the parade ground. Like most of the others, I had used my pint mug on the train journey and it was packed into the top of my kit bag. My mug was amongst those that were broken when the kit bags hit the tarmac of the parade ground.

With a lot of encouragement from the D.I.s, we eventually were lined into threes. We were told in no uncertain terms to "be quiet and listen carefully". The corporal who made this statement, we came to know as Cpl. Kent. He was holding a clipboard. "When I call your name, find your kit bag and line up over there in threes". He then started to call out names in alphabetical order. The first names to be called were 'As' and 'Bs' with a sprinkling of 'Cs'. As the first 16 picked through the pile of kit bags and started to line up, another of the D.I.s started chivvying them into place, bawling and shouting at them and calling them all sorts of names. When they had all lined up, the D.I. marched them away across the square, in the direction of the wooden huts that ran along the bottom of the parade ground. My newly found friend Ted was in the first group and the depression I was all ready feeling deepened, as I realised we were not going to be together. Slowly the numbers of us dwindled down until those that were left had names that ranged from 'S' to 'Z'. With the name Voyse, I was one of the last to be called out. Finding my kit bag was easy, as only a few were left. I picked up my kit bag, realising from the rattling sound that I had a broken mug in the top. The corporal that we were left with was Corporal Irwin, he was the smallest in stature of the D.I.s and, as we were to find out, the easiest going and friendliest of the D.I.s. His orders of command were not half as harsh as the other D.I.s we were to come into contact with.

We were marched in an untidy fashion to Hut 43 and all of us had a struggle through the hut door, loaded down as we were, with our full equipment and kit bags. My bed was the third from the bottom, on the left-hand side of the hut. Cpl. Irwin told us to dump our equipment on our beds and get our 'irons' (knives, forks and spoons), and our mugs, as he was taking us to the cookhouse. We lined up again outside the hut and marched up for our meal. I was still feeling a bit down, what with my broken mug, and having been split up from Ted, I now had to strike up new relationships with the lads in Hut 43. Only one of those who I had shared the hut with at R.A.F. Cardington was in my hut now, his name also beginning with 'V'. I was to find out later, that there was another 'Sheffielder' in Hut 43. Strangely he had travelled from Sheffield on the same day and on the same train as me, and yet I had not come across him until West Kirby, his name was Mike and he was to be responsible for the smashing of my second mug, but that comes later.

We had a meal and I was able to borrow someone else's mug to have a drink. Cpl. Irwin said that I would be able to purchase a new mug from the N.A.A.F.I..

Back in the hut, we were given our first lecture by Cpl. Irwin. We were told that we must keep our accommodation spotless and that, from the next day, our drill instruction would begin proper. We were shown how to 'square up' our blankets and told that each day we would have to strip our beds and fold up the blankets and sheets. We were to then stack them, blanket, sheet, blanket, sheet, blanket, with a folded blanket wrapped around the pile. The pile was then placed at the head of our bed and the two pillows provided were placed on the top of the pile. The mattress was covered by a fifth blanket, I had never had so much bedding before in my life. On occasions at home, we had had to make do with a couple of blankets and a coat thrown over for extra warmth.

We were instructed that there must be no direct contact between our boots or shoes and the hut floor. Cpl. Irwin showed us a piled of torn up blanket squares which we were to use as sliding mats, for use when we were manoeuvring about the hut. The floor of the hut was to be polished each day. We were told that we were expected to achieve a mirror-like shine on the floor, within the first week, using a 'bumper', which Cpl. Irwin introduced us to, showing us how to use the thing. Cpl. Irwin showed us a wall chart, which displayed the ranks of the Royal Air Force, we were at the bottom of the list, being lowly A.C.2s. "Get to know the ranks", said Cpl. Irwin, "You will learn to salute tomorrow and from then on, you will salute everyone who has the Queen's commission, from Pilot Officer upwards. We were advised to let our parents know where we were and told to write down the address. "Your address is. Hut 43, Intake 34, Flight 1, Churchill Squadron, Royal Air Force West Kirby, Larton Wirral, Cheshire", said the Corporal. What my mother thought when she saw that address I never asked. Cpl. Irwin then issued us all with a piece of circular red plastic, punched with two holes. We were instructed to place these plastic pieces behind our cap badge, the retaining pins of the badge slotting through the holes in the plastic and the holes in our berets, the whole lot being retained by a cotta-pin inside the beret.

The red plastic backing to our badges identified us as 'sprogs' (i.e. airman under training). The corporal explained that there were four squadrons at West Kirby at any one time, all named after famous people. As well as Churchill Squadron, which was ours, there were, Roosevelt, Smuts, and Trenchard. The squadron members could be identified by the colour of the plastic backing to the R.A.F. badge, blue, green and yellow, being the other colours used. Cpl. Irwin said that he wanted our hut to be the best in the squadron and warned us that the last hut on parade each day would be placed on kitchen fatigue. We did well, in eight weeks we only did fatigues twice, as will be explained later.

Before leaving us, Cpl. Irwin gave us a demonstration in cleaning our boots and shoes. The main body of the boot (or shoe) was covered in polish and then just buffed up with the polishing brush. The toe-caps were a different thing. A duster was dipped in the polish, with a finger inside the duster, and then circular movements were made on the toe-cap. This was alternated with 'spit' and then some more polish. The handle of our steel knife was to be used to smooth out the 'orange peel' effect on the toe-cap. By the end of our 8 weeks at square bashing, most of those in our hut had boots with mirror-like toe-caps, I was one of the unfortunates who had a greasy pair of boots, I was never able to achieve other than a dull shine on my boots. Even Cpl. Irwin gave up on my boots.

As he left the hut, Cpl. Irwin told us to turn in early, as we would be getting up early. He had told us the location of the ablution block and said that, in the morning, we should get washed and shaved and then get our beds made up, before making our way to the cookhouse. When walking to the cookhouse, our 'irons' and mug should be in the left hand behind our back and we should march smartly, swinging our right arm. We went to bed after a long day, absolutely tired out. Even though I was tired, I had great difficulty in getting to sleep. I must have dropped off eventually and did not seem to have been asleep very long, when I was suddenly awoken by the sound of shouting and the noise of wood banging on metal. "Wakey Wakey", "come on, let's have you" and "move yourselves", each phrase interspersed with the bang of wood against the metal bed frames. "Hands off your c...s, on to your socks".

I jumped out of bed to see a D.I. making his way down the hut, obviously enjoying himself. Within a matter of minutes we were all going to our ablutions, towels round necks and hands grasping soap, toothpaste and toothbrushes. In the ablutions block, there were rows of sinks on each side of a line of toilet doors. The walls of the W.C.s were covered in writing, mostly charts marking off the numbers of days past airmen had completed in sixes with a line across, indicating one week. Eight such rows showed that some lucky 'erk' had completed his period of square-bashing. There were one or two attempts at nude female art also on the walls. After quickly completing my ablutions, I went back to the hut, joining others who had been quicker than me, in bed making activities.

After donning my full uniform (battledress), I made my way with others to the cookhouse for breakfast. Just like the cookhouse at Cardington, the cookhouse at West Kirby always seemed to have the overriding aroma of kippers and, like every other R.A.F. cookhouse I went in, was very noisy. After having breakfast we came out, cleaning our 'irons' in the tank of scalding hot water which stood outside the cookhouse. Great care had to be taken in carrying out this operation, the bottom of the tank was littered with knives, forks and spoons, belonging to airmen who had dipped a little too deep, touched the hot water and let go of their 'irons'. I never had the misfortune of dropping my 'irons' into any cleaning tank, so I never found out how an unfortunate airman recovered his belongings.

On returning to hut 43, we found Cpl. Irwin awaiting us. He told us to put our 'irons' and mug in the hut and get straight back outside. He did not seem as friendly as the previous evening. When we had all reported back, the corporal took us up on to the parade ground, where we began the rudiments of drilling, standing to attention, standing at ease and standing easy. On other parts of the parade ground our compatriots were being given similar instructions, whilst at the far side of the square we could see more experienced airmen drilling with rifles.

And so the first morning went by with D.I.s shouting, "Atten-shun", "Stand a-a-at ease", "Stand easy", with each command being given in a long drawn out manner. Half way through the morning we had a welcome break, with a cuppa and bun being served from the N.A.A.F.I. wagon, a van with lift up sides that served refreshments. After our lunch break, we practised saluting, "longest way up, shortest way down", shouted the corporal, "the fingers of the hand level with your forehead and the palm of the hand facing the front". Everything was done by numbers, with the cry of "one-pause-two" being heard across the parade ground as we all shouted out in time with our drill movements.

Each day we had a period on the parade ground, progressing each day. We learned to march in step and to swing our arms correctly, although some unfortunate souls had great difficulty in synchronising their arm and leg movements in the correct order. They were bawled at mercilessly by the drill instructors. Worse was to come for these people for in the second week we were taken to the armoury, where we were issued with rifles and a clip of dummy bullets. The possession of these items meant more misery as it was an extra piece of equipment to clean. From the day of issue, we never went on the parade ground without the rifle. We were taught to march carrying the rifle on our shoulder, we went through the drill of standing to attention, standing at ease and standing easy, this time with the rifle.

We were shown how to present arms to officers of the rank of Squadron Leader and above, and how to do 'butt-salutes' to Flight Lieutenants and below. The difficult manoeuvre of "fix bayonets" was shown to us. We had to grab the rifle between our knees and, turning slightly to the left, draw our bayonets from the scabbard and place the blunt end, on to the fitment made for it at the end of the rifle. A number of airmen had the misfortune of dropping their rifle. There was no way of hiding this misdemeanour, as there was in other drill mistakes. Whether you were in the centre rank, with others in front of you, there was no escaping the clatter of the rifle as it hit the deck. Any airman unfortunate to drop his rifle got the full wrath of the drill instructor and often the Squadron Drill Sergeant, who invariably was standing on the edge of the parade ground, overseeing the proceedings.

Towards the end of our square-bashing, we started to get things right and we moved like clockwork. A tip given by our corporal was to put a small coin in the container that normally held the bullets, each slap of the rifle was amplified by the coins in the rifles banging against the side of the container. As well as having to clean the rifle, we had to 'blanco' the strap and polish the brass parts of the strap. 'Blanco' was a paste that we had to rub on all of our webbing kit. Although the original colour of the product was white, and was used for putting on tennis slippers and other white shoes, (hence the trade name 'Blanco', from the French 'blanc', meaning white), the paste had been produced in air force blue and khaki for our army friends. In addition to having to Blanco our webbing, all the brass buckles had to be polished with either, 'Brasso' or 'Duraglit', the second named product was the most popular with most of the airmen I knew.

Cleaning the rifles was something else. We were taught how to strip and re-assemble our rifle and we were given something called a 'pull-through', it was like a thick piece of string with a weight on the end. Some material called 'four by two' was soaked in an evil smelling oil and the 'four by two' was placed through a loop in the 'pull-through'. The weight was dropped through the open breech of the rifle and caught at the other end of the rifle barrel. The 'four by two' was then pulled through the rifle barrel, the oil soaked material lubricating and cleaning the inside of the barrel. Woe betide anyone whose rifle was lifted up by a D.I. for inspection, and was found to have a dirty rifle barrel. Great fuss was made over the slightest speck of dust. An airman was accused of being filthy and having a rifle 'full of shit'. A session on kitchen fatigues could follow such a discovery. Special attention had to be given when we had been on the rifle range, the firing of a rifle left the barrel in a really grotty condition.

On one of the days, we were taught the correct way of killing people, by the use of the bayonet. We had to run at large sacks of straw, suspended in a gallows like structure. As we ran towards our 'victim', we were made to scream at the top of our voice. What with the D.I.s shouting and our screaming, it was a real bedlam. After stabbing the suspended 'victims', we were obliged to run our bayonets through sacks laid on the floor to resemble a person in the prone position. The corporal teaching us this gentle art told us that we must keep our bayonets spotlessly clean, as it was against the 'Geneva Convention', to stab anyone with a rusty bayonet, as they could get tetanus. I was never sure whether this statement was true or whether the corporal was joshing.

Talking about tetanus, we had to receive injections and inoculations whilst at West Kirby. The day of our 'jabs' is well remembered. It was a lovely sunny day and we were all lined up outside the camp hospital on the grass. We were instructed to remove our jackets and roll up our sleeves. Along the line came the doctors and medics. Each airman was given an inoculation in the left arm, I think it was to protect us against Smallpox. In the right arm we were given a tetanus jab.

The medics issued us with documents showing the jabs we had been given and we were instructed to write our names and service number on the documents and the small blue cardboard case we were given to keep the documents in. Some airmen fainted after being given the jabs, others fainted before either of the jabs was given. In respect of the tetanus injection, we were instructed that all airmen with an even number at the end of their service number would receive their second tetanus 'booster' injection before leaving West Kirby. Those with an odd final number were told that their 'booster' would be given when they arrived at their permanent unit. I was one of those with an odd number and I must admit, like some of the others, we breathed a sigh of relief that we were to be spared a second session with the needle for some time. My good fortune in this area was not to last.

One day we were on the 'Assault Course'. On such visits to this popular venue, we were obliged to wear denim overalls to protect our main clothing from the mud, which was always prevalent on assault courses. There were many new pleasant skills to learn, climbing ropes, swinging across stretches of water, climbing walls, scrambling through dark wet and dirty tunnels, running over stretches of water on a slimy pole, and crawling under barbed wire entanglements. On this particular day we were all wearing our webbing over our denim overalls and this included our backpack.

Whilst crawling under the barbed wire I was following another airman. We were pushing our rifles in front of us and moving our arms and legs in a frog-like fashion. A strand of barbed wire caught on the backpack of the man in front of me and, as he crawled forward, it stretched out and then sprang back striking me in the forehead. A rusty prong of barbed wire stuck into my forehead, making a neat hole on the piece of skin between my eyes. I was temporarily stunned and a D.I. must have seen what had happened, for I felt myself being dragged out from under the barbed wire. There was no blood from the wound, only a hole with dirt around it and the starting of a bruise. The corporal examined me and decided to send me to the camp hospital. I was taken there in an ambulance and, on arrival, was further examined by a doctor. I was asked if I had had my tetanus injection and asked to produce my documents. Unfortunately I had left the documents back in my locker, so I received a roasting and was told that I should carry the documents on my person at all times. I was given a booster shot of tetanus and told that, at the earliest opportunity, I was to report to the hospital with my documents to have them marked up. Such was life at square-bashing camp that I never got around to this task, with the result that I received further injections at RAF Warton hospital, despite my protestations (see p.28).

On the occasions when we had to do kitchen fatigues, we were put in a shed with open sides and large metal sinks. We were given what seemed to be hundreds of dirty, greasy, pans to clean, the pile never seemed to reduce. The tepid water was horrible, there was a crust of floating grease on the top of the water, and a 'tide mark' of grease extended up our arms, as we tried to de-grease the pans. It was freezing cold in the open sided shed and we seemed to be there forever. The second visit on kitchen fatigues was spent peeling potatoes. I had seen such scenes in movie films about the army, but never envisaged that one day I would be doing the same. Thankfully I was only chosen once for each of the above charming activities.

Rushing to make sure our hut was not the last on parade caused me to injure myself and caused me some embarrassment. Like many of my compatriots, shaving was a new experience to me. Everybody had the 'safety' type razors and used a brush and shaving cream or shaving soap to lather the face. The water was never very hot and shaving in a hurry meant that one could easily sustain a shaving cut. One morning whilst shaving, I gave myself a real deep cut, on the left hand side of my chin, so deep that I bear the scar to this day. I really ought to have had a stitch put in the wound, but I hurried up and finished shaving, washing the lather off of my face, and the blood, with cold water.

I got a piece of toilet paper and held it to my face, putting pressure on the cut. I managed somehow to collect up my toiletries and went back to the hut, where someone suggested that a piece of newspaper was the done thing on a shaving cut. I stuck a piece of newspaper on the cut and put on my shirt and my collar and tie and battledress jacket. Before leaving the hut, I changed the piece of newspaper, replacing it with a fresh chunk. Grabbing my rifle, I joined the rest of my colleagues on the parade ground, where we lined up in columns of three. One of the D.I.s, a Corporal hailing from Scotland, was chivvying us into line and eventually gave the order, 'Atten-shun', we all stood stiffly to attention. The Drill Sergeant, who was a dead ringer for the late Sidney James, stood towards the centre of the parade ground as the erks from each hut were lined up by the D.I.s. As we stood there the Corporals started walking through the ranks, inspecting each airman.

Various comments came out like:

'Have you had a haircut recently airman?'

To which the unfortunate erk would say, 'Yes Corporal.'

'WELL GET ANOTHER!' the D.I. would shout.

Or perhaps…

'Did you use a mirror to shave with this morning airman?'

'Yes Corporal.'

'WELL NEXT TIME USE A BLEEDING RAZOR!'

The Scottish Corporal made his way along the line in which I stood, making some malicious comment about everyone or some sarcastic quip. Eventually, he arrived directly in front of me, looked me up and down, and, spotting the piece of newspaper stuck to my chin, stood right up to me so close, that his nose was nearly touching mine.

'SERGEANT!' he shouted, 'WE'VE GOT A FUNNY MAN HERE, HE'S GOT HALF OF THE 'NEWS OF THE WORLD' STUCK TO HIS FACE!'

I was as red as a beetroot. The Sergeant marched up, stick under his left arm and looked at me, saying, 'Try not to stand too close to the razor next time son', the Corporal with a satisfied grin on his face moved on to the next unfortunate.

Another funny incident involving the Scottish corporal occurred one day when, once again on the parade, the squadron sergeant gave us a lecture on the amount of graffiti in the ablutions block, although I don't think the word 'graffiti' was used. Anyway the sergeant left us in no doubt as to what we would suffer if the graffiti wasn't removed. After the lecture we were marched off the parade ground. As we marched our Scottish friend recited the following ditty, 'It is a man with no ambition at all, who writes his name on the shit-house wall'.

Some of the drill instructors were real 'bar stewards'. They would single out individuals and make their lives a misery. One lad, Fretwell, was blessed with a face that bore a permanent grin. He grinned if he was enjoying himself, he grinned if he was in pain and he grinned when he was under stress. On one occasion, he was dragged off the parade ground by a DI, who set into him something awful.

'Take that stupid grin off your face Fretwell', shouted the corporal.

Well of course the poor lad couldn't. The more the DI shouted at him, the more he grimaced, his face set in a hurt grin. The more he grinned, the angrier the DI appeared to get. We felt sorry for Fretwell, but could do nothing to help him. He finished up on kitchen fatigues because he could not stop grinning.

Another time, South, the only married man in our unit, was being 'got at' by the same DI. Suddenly the DI made some derogatory remark referring to South's wife. Suddenly South broke rank and grabbed hold of the DI by the front of his jacket, nearly lifting him off the ground. His left hand was clenched into a fist and he made as though to strike the corporal. He suddenly realised what he was doing and luckily he held back. The DI was visibly shaken. We all thought that South would be in serious trouble, however, the incident never went any further and the DI stopped picking on South.

On one occasion, I was chosen to be the 'Duty Runner' for the day. I was instructed to report to the Squadron office, wearing my battledress and webbing belt. I spent the day either sitting in the foyer outside the main office, or going to various parts of the camp with envelopes. I got to see parts of the camp I had not previously seen, and was enjoying my bit of freedom. I was walking alongside one of the parade grounds, when suddenly something that sounded like 'YEOMAN' echoed in my direction. I stopped in my tracks. A Warrant Officer came towards me shouting.

'WHO THE BLOODY HELL DO YOU THINK YOU ARE? BUFFALO BILL?'

I had no idea what to answer and just blankly looked at the Warrant Officer.

'Look at that webbing belt Yeoman, get the thing straightened up, it looks like a cowboys belt with the gun missing.'

I looked down and my webbing belt was slightly down on the left-hand side. I straightened it up quickly.

'That's better young man, and swing your arms when you are marching around the camp'.

Not sure what to do next, I said 'Yes sir!', and threw up a salute. Of course only commissioned officers warranted a salute and a Warrant Officer does not hold a commission. This was explained to me in no uncertain terms by the gentleman who had stopped me! I was then told to get on my way, with a final, 'Be more careful in future yeoman'.

The rest of the day I felt uncomfortable, continually looking over my shoulder and dreading meeting anyone coming towards me. For some considerable time in the early days of my service, I continued to experience difficulty in differentiating between the cap badge of a Warrant Officer and that of a commissioned officer.

On some weekends we were able to get out of camp, travelling in large groups to Birkenhead, Liverpool or New Brighton. Liverpool was a very busy port at that time and there were lots of people walking the streets in all types of uniform. It was a nightmare for us 'sprogs'; we didn't know who to salute and who not to salute. If we were in doubt we slung up a salute to be safe. I think we must have saluted Bus Inspectors, Cinema Commissioners and many others in our ignorance of the ranks of the services. The trips out to these places meant using the electric railway, which ran from the aforementioned places to West Kirby and back. For some reason, we always alighted at a station called Meols, from where we used taxis to take us to the camp gates. The taxis were something else. They were large American cars and we all piled into them, some erks standing on the running boards for the short journey between the station and the camp gates. I remember it was 1/6d in old money for the short journey, those taxi drivers must have made a fortune over the years that R.A.F. West Kirby was open as a square bashing camp.

On a couple of occasions we went on the electric railway to the seaside town of New Brighton. Like many seaside towns, New Brighton had plenty of attractions for young people. On one occasion we were in an amusement arcade when one of the lads found a slot machine which was faulty. It was one of those machines on which you flicked a curved lever and sent a ball bearing spinning around curved metal strips and hopefully into one of the slots marked 'WIN'. On this machine, even when the ball went into the slot marked 'LOST', the ball was returned. We crowded around the machine until it was emptied of Halfpenny coins.

We found a backstreet café, where we enjoyed steak and chips. The proprietor asked us to recommend his establishment to our mates, which we said we would. In return, he piled our plates with food.

On one occasion, me and one of my mates, met up with two girls who were on a day trip, we spent the afternoon with them, going on all the rides and generally enjoying our selves. At the end of the afternoon, we walked the girls back to the coach park and stood at the back of the coach with our arms around the girls, exchanging kisses, in full view of their interested friends who were all ready on the coach. Suddenly an adult came to the rear of the coach and said to the girls, 'Are you coming or what?, the coach drivers wanting to get off'. The girls reluctantly left us and boarded the coach waving to us. It was only after the coach had left that we both realised that we had not got the girl's addresses, all we knew about them was their first names. Ships that pass in the night!

Midway through our training, we were allowed a 48 hour leave pass, (I still have the leave form, made out as instructed by Cpl Irwin, and signed by an officer). I was one of the lucky ones who could get home without difficulty for the 48-hour pass and travelled home via Liverpool and Manchester. I felt very proud, but strange, walking up our road on my first home leave.

During my weekend at home I went round my friends and relations, showing myself off. It was not unusual to see lads in uniform on the city streets at that time of National Service and the sight of a serviceman in uniform was common, right up to the start of the 'troubles' in Northern Ireland flaring up again in the Sixties. On my visits around Sheffield, I was accompanied by my mate Mick, who was soon to be wearing the blue uniform of the R.A.F. himself. The weekend was soon over and Mick accompanied me to the Victoria station in Sheffield, where I caught a train to Manchester. At Manchester I changed to a train for Liverpool, and then, on arrival in Liverpool. I transferred on to the electric railway for the final part of the journey back to West Kirby. Going back was a bit of a drag and I was not looking forward to picking up where we had left off prior to our 48-hour pass. On the electric train there were a number of returning airmen, including Mick from Sheffield, who strangely enough I had not bumped into at any point during the return journey, on the other trains.

When I finally arrived back at our hut, I spent some time chatting with the others about what we had been doing over the weekend. We felt sorry for some of the lads who had not been able to go home, like Jock, a bit of a bumpkin from Scotland. Jock, like many of us had never been far from his home and had never been into England before. His accent was very strong and we all had difficulty in understanding him. There were others from the extremities of the country that had spent their 48-hour pass in the Camp. After a short while it was down to our 'bulling' duties, ready for the following day.

Whilst we were unpacking our small-kit, someone noticed that Mick had an R.A.F. badge painted on his mug. Everyone gathered around to examine the work of art, various people expressed admiration of the badge asking Mick who had decorated his mug. Mick proudly told everyone that, in 'civvie' street he was a sign writer by trade, having served a five-year apprenticeship. Mick looked, and was indeed, older than most of us in the hut. People started asking Mick if he could paint them something on their pint-pot and over the next few days, in between bouts of his 'bulling' duties, Mick obliged for a small fee. I was one who had a cartoon character painted on the side of my mug. I thought it looked great.

Friday night was kit inspection night and the hut had to be really 'bulled' to perfection and our kit laid out on our bed for inspection. Everything had to be precisely in order, as shown by a large photograph on a wall poster. Blankets were folded meticulously, as explained previously and every item of kit laid out in its specific place on the bed. The floor of the hut shone and hopefully, there was not a speck of dust to be found. The coalbunker and the stove were blacked and shone, and the top of the coalbunker was painted white. The brush and bumper handles were scraped white with a razor blade and we hoped against hope that everything was as it should be. Eventually the senior man in the hut shouted, 'Officer present, stand by your beds'. We all stood smartly to attention as an officer and a sergeant entered the hut.

Starting at the first bed on the right, the pair looked carefully at the neatly arranged equipment. Suddenly, the sergeant grabbed hold of the cane, which he had under his left arm and pushed the cane through the handle of the pint-pot which lay in the centre of the bed surrounded by the airman's 'irons'.

Lifting the mug up into the air with the cane, he said, 'This is nice, who's done this'.

Mick stepped forward one step and proudly said, 'Me sergeant!'

The sergeant tilted his cane and the pint-pot slid slowly down the cane and crashed onto the floor. Mick's face turned to a brilliant red, the rest of us who had had our mugs decorated had a look of fear and apprehension on our faces as we knew what to expect. The sergeant made his way down the hut picking up each decorated mug and throwing it to the ground, the officer looked on in approval. Not only did we get our mug broken, we had to clean up the mess made, and finished up on kitchen fatigue for the second time. Mick was very embarrassed by the whole affair.

Later the sergeant had the cheek to ask Mick to paint an R.A.F. coat of arms on the entrance door to the Sergeants Mess. It was necessary to purchase a further mug from the N.A.A.F.I., this time my mug remained in its original condition for the rest of my service.

Another episode involving Mick was when we were on an exercise. The whole of the camp was split into two 'armies'. We were all in denims and had to wear a coloured ribbon on our shoulder tabs, you were either in the 'red army' or the 'blue army'. Prior to the commencement of the exercise, we were in large groups being issued with various pieces of equipment, like sten-guns or bren-guns. Whilst we were standing around awaiting instructions, Mick noticed an airman standing with his back to the others, this airman was in denims, exactly as we were, and was wearing a beret. He had no coloured ribbon on his shoulder. Mick went up behind him and, in his broad Sheffield accent said, 'Na then kid, whose side are thy on?'

You can imagine the look on Mick's face, when the 'kid' turned around and we all saw the embroidered badge of an officer on his beret. Mick didn't ask any further questions that day. During the exercise, the 'blue army' left the camp in lorries and we, the 'red army' had the task of defending the camp from attack. I spent a long period in a ditch, on the outside of the perimeter fence, with another airman and a sergeant. We 'captured' a small group of attacking troops led by a corporal. As we lay concealed in the ditch, we saw the group coming along our side of the hedge, which surrounded the field we were in.

They were all running at the stoop, using the hedge for cover. Unfortunately they were on the wrong side of the hedge. We waited until they were almost on top of us and then opened fire with blanks. Even though we were only three, it was counted as a capture. We led the disgruntled corporal and his group back into the camp, they were 'blue' in more ways than one.

During the exercise we had a break for refreshments. Our mess tins came into proper use for the first time. The tins were rectangular aluminium containers, with folding handles, one was slightly smaller than the other, which enabled the smaller one to fit into the larger one, with the handles folded over. Up to that point we had only cleaned them and displayed them on 'bull' nights. We queued up for the food which was being dished out and were served 'bangers and mash' in the large mess tin, and our small one was used for drinking purposes, tea being dispensed from a large urn. When the tea was put into the small mess tin, a white scum floated to the top, this must have been the 'Brasso' which we had used to clean the tins in preparation for 'bull' night. I tried to get rid of the scum on the top of the tea, but like everyone, I was thirsty and hungry and consumed the food and drink, 'Brasso' or no 'Brasso'.

It was never officially announced who 'won', but we assumed that the camp had been successfully defended.

We had only been at West Kirby about one week, when the rumour went about that, Brian, the sexy young man at Cardington, had been sent off to the military hospital at Winchester, with a nasty disease. We certainly never saw him again and we were told that, anyone who contracted venereal disease and was taken into hospital for treatment had his service suspended for the duration of his stay in hospital. Brian therefore would have had to restart his square-bashing along with a later intake and would not necessarily have returned to West Kirby.

We progressed through our training and the instructors seemed to find some new gem every day, we learned to strip and re-assemble a Bren gun, and the less complicated Sten gun. We learned to identify the horizon by the clock, i.e., a target was said to be at 2 O'clock on the horizon or say 10 O'clock and the instructors used large paintings of landscapes to teach us this new skill. We had lectures on venereal disease, with gory photographs and films. Some of the lads fainted.

Most of us were virgins although there was a lot of bragging done. At that time most teenagers were innocent of the ways of the world, 'Lady Chatterley's Lover' was still in the abridged version and the famous trial for pornography in respect of the book was in the future. One of the best surprises was saved to the last, our visit to the gas chamber. We had heard rumours of this part of the training, older brothers had warned us of the niceties of the visit to the gas chamber. It was with some trepidation therefore that we assembled outside a single storey brick building. A corporal issued us all with gas masks and we were given a talk on how a gas mask worked. All this took place on the grass outside the aforementioned building. Eventually amidst nervous laughter, we were instructed to don our gas masks.

The corporal came round checking each gas mask, tightening up the head straps where necessary and the tightness of the rubber against the face. Eventually a group of about twenty of us was led inside the building, The interior of the building was quite bright and once inside the doors were closed. We immediately became aware of a canister, about the size of a two-pint tin of paint in the centre of the building, there was smoke emitting from the canister in a strong upward jet. The corporal's muffled voice and his hand signals prompted us into forming a rectangular circle around the edge of the room.

We then started to march around the room about an arms length apart and did about three laps of the circle. We then received the signal to remove our gas masks. The natural reaction was to take a deep breath before removing the gas mask. Once the masks were off we recommenced marching around the circle.

Most people tried to hold their breath, including me, but eventually we were forced to exhale. The next intake was of gas and was a strong inhalation of the gas. We all started coughing and spluttering.

We had been instructed outside that, once our masks were off we were to place our right hand on the shoulder of the man in front. This was because, not only were we coughing and spluttering, our eyes were streaming and we could not see. We tramped around the room, stumbling. It seemed to go on forever and I lost count of the number of revolutions we did. Suddenly the door opened and we all literally fell out of the building, collapsing in heaps on the grass. The fresh air was beautiful and greatly appreciated by all. It took some time for our eyes to clear and everyone looked as though they had had a heavy weeping session, eyes were red and noses running. What was it all about?, we were told it was to give us confidence in our gas mask. It certainly gave me an appreciation of fresh air.

As we reached the end of our square-bashing, our drill movements became more and more slick, we all moved as one as each command was given. Our arms and legs moved in co-ordination and to put it bluntly, we were very smart. We started to practise for our passing out parade, the whole of the squadron marching together, rifles at the slope. On reaching the spot where the saluting base would be, we were given the 'EYES RIGHT' command, everyone, with the exception of the man at the very front-right, known as the right marker, looked over their right shoulder until the order 'EYES FRONT', was given. To a man we all returned our gaze to the front. It was a hard movement to master, it was easy to catch the heel of the man in front. We were marching without any forward vision for about twenty to thirty steps, whilst trying to balance a heavy rifle on the left shoulder. After some initial mistakes we could do the drill like clockwork.

The night before the passing out parade, was one of frantic 'bulling'. Trousers had to have a knife-edge crease, buttons and buckles were shone until they gleamed like gold. The cap and its badge were brushed and polished respectively, and the boots were black and shiny. Rifles were cleaned and the webbing straps 'blancoed', the clips of brass were polished. Our 'Best Blue' uniforms were hung up carefully that night and our caps were placed on the shelf of our lockers with great care.

The next morning was bright and clear and, after breakfast, we all lined up outside our individual huts, resplendent in our 'Best Blue'. Our drill corporal then closely inspected us. He was also turned out immaculately. It was the first time we had seen him in his 'Best Blue' and he looked impressive. Round his shoulder he wore a red sash which hung below his left arm and finished in a tassel. Under his arm he carried a drill cane. Every individual airman was given the 'once-over'. Ties were straightened, caps placed correctly on the head, bits were picked from the uniform serge and we were looked up and down, front and back.

The corporal had a duster, with which he touched up buttons, rubbed badges and gave a final polish to boots. When he was reasonably satisfied he shouted, 'SQUAD', to which we all stiffened. 'SQUAD, AAATTENSHUN', we all stood smartly to attention, with our rifles close up to our left legs. The next command was, 'RIGHT DRESS', we all shuffled our feet and put our right arm up on to shoulder of the man immediately to the right, heads tilted stiffly to the right, as we had been taught. 'EYES FRONT', we looked to the front and at the same time slammed our right arms into the right leg.

The next command was, 'SQUAAAD, SLOPE ARMS'. As one we all lifted our rifles up into the slope arms position. Then came the command, 'LEFT TURN', again we all moved in unison, turning left in columns of three. We stood there for a few moments whilst the corporal had a quick walk up and down us. Outside the other huts, our colleagues were all ready to move off. The corporal marched smartly to the head of our group and took up his position.

We then heard a different voice, which was loud enough to be heard along the whole of the lines. 'CHURCHILL SQUADRON! BY THE LEFT, QUICK MARCH!' . We started to march toward the Drill Square and as we approached we became aware of the audience, made up of invited guests, proud parents, and senior officers, who were all seated at the bottom side of the square facing the parade ground. At the topside of the parade ground towards the middle was the band. As we approached the parade ground the band struck up the Royal Air Force march-past music, a strange tingle of pride ran down my spine as we marched onto the square and were brought to a halt, perfectly lined up in front of the audience, with an equal amount of space on each side of the Squadron.

The order was given to turn to the right, followed by the command to order arms. We were given the order move in to open order. The middle rank stood their ground, whilst the front and rear ranks moved one step forward and back respectively. The 'RIGHT DRESS' command was given and we all did our shuffling bit with the right arm extended on to our neighbours shoulder and heads to the right. 'EYES FRONT' came the command, we all stood smartly to attention facing the audience. A high ranking officer, with thick blue bands on the bottom of his sleeve left the podium on which he had been stood and, accompanied by an officer of a lower rank strolled across toward the left of the lined up airmen.

The band struck up a nice melody that was conducive to the strolling movements of the officers. Slowly but surely the officers came along the front ranks, stopping every so often to speak to an individual airman. As they approached me, I braced myself in case they spoke to me, they passed me by, simply looking at me and stopped at the airman next but one from me. I could not hear what was being said.

When they reached the end of the front rank and moved into the middle rank, the order, 'FRONT AND REAR RANK, STAND AT EASE!' came, we all stood at ease with our rifles sloping forward and our legs apart. The inspection continued for what seemed an age. As the officers got close to the end of the centre rank, the rear rank was brought to attention and then the centre rank was brought to the 'stand at ease' position, whilst the rear rank was inspected. Shortly before the officers reached the end of the inspection, the front and centre ranks were brought back to attention.

The band continued to play the 'strolling' type music until the officers arrived back at the podium and stood facing the massed ranks of airmen. The music stopped abruptly and the order came to 'slope arms', followed the command, PARADE!, LEFT TURN!. We all turned as commanded. As the band struck up a marching tune, we were given the order to 'quick march' and we moved off, doing a full circuit of the parade ground, around the top side of the band and then eventually along the bottom of the parade ground. As we approached the podium the order came to, 'EYES RIGHT', we all did our bit as we had been taught looking towards the officers on the podium, who were stood at attention saluting the parade. I can remember the tune that was playing as we marched past, it was the famous tune, 'Sussex by the Sea', why that tune was chosen for a parade taking place by the side of the River Mersey, I'll never know.

We did a full circuit again and on the second passing of the podium we were brought to the slow march, the band playing an appropriate slow tune. As the last group cleared the podium, the tune changed to a 'quick march' and we received the order to quicken our step. On reaching the bottom of the parade ground, we were brought to a halt, turned to face the audience and given the command to 'order arms'. The high ranking officer gave a final salute and then proceeded to leave the podium followed by an entourage of lesser ranking officers. Once they had cleared the area, the order to 'stand at ease' was given, followed quickly by the 'stand easy' command. We stood in that fashion for a short while, before being brought back to attention followed by the blessed command, 'PARADE!, DISMISS'. We all did a quarter turn to the left and the passing out parade was over. Most of us breathed a sigh of relief; it had seemed to last forever. Those airmen whose parents had been able to attend made their way over to their family and friends, whilst those of us who were not so lucky, stood around in groups talking excitedly. The weeks of drilling and bulling were over, we now felt a part of the Royal Air Force. I wished that I had been fortunate, as others were to have had photographs taken of the parade, soon we would all be split asunder as we were posted to different trade training units up and down the United Kingdom. I was never again to see, the majority of the people with whom I had spent the last eight weeks.

The following day, our last at RAF West Kirby, we all paraded outside the Squadron office informally, the various drill instructors came out of the offices, with bundles of documents and we all gathered around our individual corporal. The corporal started shouting out names and proceeded to dish out the documents he had in his hand, a buzz of excitement went around as we realised we were being given the information of what trade we had been allocated for our time with the RAF. Eventually my name was called and I feverishly looked at the papers I had been given. My trade was designated as 'Fighter Plotter/Radar

Operator' and my orders were that, following my end of square-bashing leave of one week, I was to report to RAF Middle Wallop, in Hampshire, for trade training. Rail warrants for the journey to Sheffield and from Sheffield to Andover were in the bundle of documents. We spent the next hour comparing notes with one another and I found out that the only other airman who I knew, that was to go to RAF Middle Wallop, was Chris from Dewsbury.

That night we had a bit of a fling in the NAAFI, there was much shaking of hands and exchanging of addresses as the evening came to a close. We had been instructed by our corporal to empty ashes from the dustbin on to the hut floor and to slide around in our boots to take the shine off the floor, life was not going to be easy for the next intake. Although I took part in the ritual, I did it with some unease.

And so our time at RAF West Kirby came to an end. It had been a traumatic time, but I think we all benefited from the experience in the long term. We had been turned from a bumbling mass, into smart well-drilled airmen. The self-discipline taught would stand us in good stead for the rest of our lives. We went on leave and a week later a new adventure started.

4. RAF Middle Wallop

(In which I become a plotter)

Travelling home via Liverpool and Manchester, I finally arrived at the Victoria Station, in Sheffield, the former Great Central railway station which later became the L.N.E.R. (London and North Eastern Railway) and finally the British Railways (Eastern Region) station for Sheffield. The station no longer exists, the Sheffield to Manchester line via the Woodhead tunnel being closed in the 1960s.

When I got out on to the station approach, I found it was pouring with rain. Not being affluent enough to afford a taxi, I walked down the station approach road, across the centre of town, to the tram stop outside the central post office in Flat Street. I was carrying my full kit. Webbing belt and straps with pouches attached at the front, my backpack, stuffed with various items of uniform, bayonet scabbard and water bottle and my kit bag slung over my shoulder. I finally reached the tram stop where I joined the queue awaiting the tram for Woodseats.

Standing under the tram shelter, I saw a lady selling flowers, she was a regular at this spot and I had seen her many times before. Whilst waiting, I had the brilliant idea of taking a bunch of flowers home for my mother. I had a struggle extracting some money from my pocket, without putting my kit bag on to the wet and dirty pavement, but managed to do so. I selected a nice bunch of flowers and paid for them, rejoining the tram queue. Flat Street was very busy, it was the beginning of the evening rush hour. There I stood holding my kit bag with my left hand

and a bunch of flowers in my right hand, suddenly a woman came past with an umbrella in her hand, as she passed me by, her umbrella knocked my hat off on to the dirty wet pavement. Being on a hill, my hat rolled about twenty to thirty feet. I just stood there for a few moments watching it roll down the hill, before leaving the queue and giving chase. Another lady saw my predicament and bent down and collected my hat, plonking it untidily on my head, I was unable to adjust it and so again joined the queue with the feeling that my hat was going to fall off again at the slightest movement of my head.

The tram eventually arrived and I boarded and took a seat in the lower saloon, sitting on the edge of the seat, due to the backpack pushing me forward, my kit bag on the floor of the tram and my bunch of flowers across my knee. I finally reached home and was welcomed warmly by my mother and my sister, who had just arrived home from work. My mother then said, what was later to become a standing joke every time I came home on leave, "When do you go back?"

I really enjoyed my evening meal and it felt strange to be sleeping in my own bed that night. Lying in the next morning was sheer luxury.

The week at home passed really fast. I spent most of my time with my friend Mick Dickinson in the evenings, mostly at the local cinemas. During the day whilst Mick was at work, I went around my friends and relations, showing off in my 'best blue' uniform. At my former places of work, I tried to impress the girls, but rather than secure a date with any of them, I collected a number of addresses and promised that I would write to them. Home telephones were very few and far between in those days, so writing letters was the way of communicating with family and friends.

At the end of my leave I left home again, carrying my full kit and waving goodbye to my Mum as I went down the road. Again I was full of apprehension, I had a long journey in front of me. My rail warrant was made out to Andover in Hampshire and that was the furthest I had ever been from home. The first part of my journey was quite all right, I was travelling from Sheffield Midland station to St. Pancras station in London.

I had never been to London before and I had been told at Sheffield station that my train for Andover was scheduled to depart from Paddington station. This would mean that I would have to use the London underground railway. I alighted at St. Pancras and followed the crowds to the exit barriers. The ticket inspector at the barrier looked at my ticket and said something that I could not understand, clipped my ticket and gave it back to me. I was swept along with the crowd, before I could ask what he had said. I saw the signs pointing to the underground railway and descended the stairs, making my way along underground corridors, looking in panic for some sign that would put me in the right direction for Paddington station.

Somehow or other I passed the barriers into the underground station and walked towards the moving escalator. When I stepped on to the moving stairway, I was nearly thrown off my balance, and then when the moving platform went over the top of the staircase, I nearly fell forward at the shock of the steepness of the staircase. At the bottom of the stairs there were further corridors to negotiate and eventually I saw another uniformed railway employee.

I stopped him and said, "excuse me, which train do I need for Paddington."

His reply was unintelligible, every other word being interspersed with "moite" – which I took to be "mate".

More by luck than judgement I eventually arrived at Paddington station and then a further dilemma commenced; I couldn't find from which platform the Andover train started. When I eventually found the correct platform, I found that a train to Andover had just departed and I had an hour to wait for the next. I was close to tears. Eventually the next train arrived and I boarded.

The train had green carriages and for the first time in my life I travelled on the southern region of British Railways. The journey to Andover is a blur and lost in my memory, I do however remember alighting at Andover station and spotting another 'Erk', also with full kit, making his way towards the station exit. I hurried after him and asked him if he was bound for R.A.F. Middle Wallop. He said 'Yes'. I asked if he knew his way from Andover and was disappointed when he said 'No'. He suggested that we both get a taxi and share the fare. Although I knew I couldn't really afford such a luxury, I was by this time desperately tired and agreed.

We arrived at the gates of Royal Air Force Middle Wallop, alighted from the taxi and made our way to the guardroom. A sinister looking S.P. greeted us; he had a scar all the way down one cheek. Whilst at the station I got to know this RAF policeman a bit more, but that comes later. Needless to say he was known as 'scarface' to all and sundry, and he was sadly lacking in humour.

He looked at our documents, which contained our travel and training course joining instructions. "You're late", he said, looking directly at me. I started to explain the difficulties I had encountered in London, when he interrupted me in mid sentence. "Wait there, both of you".

He turned and went into the guardroom and from the outside I heard him mention my name and number and that of my new found friend. I then heard the sound of a telephone being replaced in its cradle and then the sound of the policeman's boots on the polished floor of the guardroom entrance corridor. "If you hang on there someone will show you to your billet", he said. He turned on his heel and disappeared back into the guardroom. We stood there like two 'stuffed ducks', both holding our kit bags in front of us, for what seemed an age.

Suddenly an airman, with the insignia of a Leading Aircraftman on his arm, walked up.

"You Voyse and McKintyre?"

We nodded.

"Follow me."

We picked up our kit bags and duly followed him towards some 'H' block buildings.

"Where you from?", he said, looking at me.

"Sheffield" I said.

"And you?" he said to McKintyre.

"Stirling sir!" said McKintyre, in a soft Scottish accent.

"Blimey! Don't call me sir," said our guide.

The rest of the way to the 'H' block he spent asking us whether we were regulars and what trade we were. When we said we were training to become Radar Operator/Fighter Plotters, he simply said, "Oh". We entered the 'H' block and climbed the stairs to the first floor.

I was suitably impressed, this was a vast improvement on the hut accommodation we had experienced at Cardington and West Kirby.

"Wait there Voyse," said our guide.

McKintyre was shown into a room on the right hand side of the building, whilst I was taken to the left. As we walked along the corridor towards the room, the LAC said, "There's the ablutions", pointing to a room on the right, "And there's the laundry and ironing room", he said, pointing to the left. "The cookhouse is, out of the door, turn left and then left again and straight down the path, the food's not bad here".

He showed me into a dormitory room on the left at the end of the corridor, taking me to a vacant bedspace. He said, "See you around," turned and disappeared out of the room. I never saw him again.

I started unpacking my kit and stowing it away in the large and small lockers, to the left hand side of the bed. I had just about hung everything up, or placed items on the shelves and in the one drawer, when I heard a voice behind me say, "Voyse".

I turned around and immediately stiffened; it was a corporal. I stood to attention. "Relax lad," said the corporal. He then explained that he was one of the course instructors. "Get yourself a meal and settle yourself in for the night, everyone on the course will parade on the drill square tomorrow morning at 8 o'clock. Don't be late. I'll see you tomorrow."

"Thank you corporal," I said. The corporal turned and left the room, that was when I relaxed. As I finished stowing the last of my kit away, airmen started drifting into the room in ones and twos. Several of them nodded to me and then started to get their irons and pots out of their lockers.

"Do you know where the cookhouse is?" asked one lad.

"I think so…" I replied hesitantly.

"Get your irons, and we'll show you the way," he said.

On the way to the cookhouse the usual, "Where are you from?" question was asked; I told them.

"Oh, Levy, in the next bed to where you are is from Sheffield, he's a Jew you know". I nodded.

One of the airmen said, "You sprogs should be in the huts down the bottom of the airfield, all together, but they are decorating them, that's why you're all mixed in with us."

"Oh!" I said.

We arrived at the cookhouse, which was in a large brick built building. When we entered, the first thing I noticed was that there were WAAFs (members of the Women's Royal Air Force) sitting at some of the tables, the first I had seen since joining the air force.

We joined the queue and shuffled to the serving counter, there seemed to be a wider choice of food here than we had had at West Kirby. The cooks behind the counter were dishing out the pointed selections of each airman, under the supervision of a very matronly looking WAAF sergeant.

When my turn came I pointed to what I wanted and received a very generous portion of everything I chose. I followed my roommates to a table and put down my plate.

"Teas over there", one of them said. "Shall I bring you some?"

"Yes please, thanks", I said. I began my meal, which was very tasty. During the meal I was asked where I had done my square-bashing and what my number was, etc., I felt accepted and was enjoying myself for the first time. All around me were airmen with different insignia on their sleeves, LACs, SACs, Junior Technicians, people with patches on showing a hand gripping flashes of lightning, it was all very interesting.

"Come on, let's get our pudding," said one of the lads. I followed them, coming back with a bowl full of pudding covered with lashings of custard. If this was what food was like here, I was certainly going to enjoy myself.

I walked back to the 'H' block with the others.

"By the way... you don't have to wear your beret here whilst you are walking between buildings," said one of the lads, "Just shove it tidily under your epaulette with the badge to the front." I took my beret off and followed their example. For some strange reason, I had not noticed that I was the only one in the small group wearing my beret.

When I got back to the dormitory, the lad who I now knew was Levy was sitting on his bed, writing pad in hand, busily writing away.

"Hey, Levy," said one of the lads. "This kid's from Sheffield."

I nodded at Levy.

"What part?" asked Levy, looking at me and raising his eyebrows.

"Heeley," I said.

"Oh," he said, going back to his writing.

"What part are you from?" I asked.

"Ecclesall," he replied, naming a rather 'posh' part of Sheffield. He continued to write and for the rest of the night ignored me.

I took my boots off and started to clean them, the dormitory was fairly full by this time and there were many conversations going off. I felt a bit left out now and concentrated on cleaning my boots. Later one of the lads who had been in the cookhouse with me came across and asked.

"Would you like to see where the NAAFI is?"

I said "Yes" and followed him and some others to the NAAFI, where we stayed for a couple of hours. I returned to the dormitory dog-tired, went to the ablutions, washed, cleaned my teeth etc. and then turned in. As I lay in my bed in these strange surroundings, with airmen still chattering away all around me, I reflected on what a hectic day I had experienced. The lights were still on when I fell asleep. I remember waking up during the night and wondering where I was, looking towards the open door of the dormitory to the dimly lit corridor.

The next morning I was woken by people around me engaged in various activities, some were making up their beds, others were wandering off with towels round their neck towards the dormitory exit door. I looked at my watch, it was about 6.25 am, I climbed out of bed got my soap, towel, toothbrush and toothpaste and joined the 'erks' at their ablutions.

After a hearty breakfast, I reported to the parade ground at the time instructed and saw about twenty other 'erks' all milling about, I looked amongst them and eventually located Jock. We stood around talking and exchanging experiences until a corporal walked up. 'Right lads, form up in threes' he shouted, we all complied with his request. We were all expecting to be brought to attention, as we had been taught at square-bashing, but the corporal simply said, 'OK everybody, left turn, quick march!'. We all started to march, following the corporal, down the camp roads and beyond the line of the permanent buildings. To our right we could see the aircraft hangars, with real aeroplanes stood on the concrete outside. I thought, 'this is the real thing now' and got quite excited, looking forward to our day's activities.

About halfway between the permanent buildings and the hangars, were some modern pre-fabricated huts. We marched to the side of one of the huts where the corporal brought us to a halt and then told us to, 'fall out'. He then said 'follow me lads' and disappeared into the nearest hut, we all filed in behind him. Once inside, we turned to the right and entered a classroom. It was neat, clean and tidy, with a green chalkboard at the front and a table and chair facing the tables and chairs on which we were asked to sit.

The corporal explained that we were to learn about the various types of radar in use in the RAF at that time. He picked up a pile of blue exercise books which had the letters 'Royal Air Force - Notebook' printed on the front cover, with an identifying code number printed in the top right hand corner. The corporal slammed the books on one of the first row tables, and instructed, 'pass those round', he then went to a filing cabinet and got out a bundle of pencils and these were passed around the class also. A short talk followed on the history of radar, and how it had helped us to defeat the German Luftwaffe, in the Second World War. We were then instructed to write notes, from the script that he was writing in chalk on the green chalkboard, complete with drawings. As he wrote the corporal was talking, his drawings of radar masts, such as the 'Chain Home' (CH) and 'Chain Home Long' (CHL) 'Ground Control Approach' (GCA) and on to the modern (at that time) American FPS3, were a lot better than the attempts I made to draw in my exercise book. We found the information very interesting and everyone gave 100% attention to the corporal.

We spent five days in the classroom and learned a lot about the trade to which we had been allocated, We copied down the phonetic alphabet and were told that we needed to commit it to memory. We drew radar screens in our books and 'blips' on the screens to represent aircraft picked up by the radar. We learned about 'IFF' (Identification Friend or Foe), being told that all RAF aircraft were fitted with a device which reflected the radar beam and caused a small 'v' shape to appear under the blip on the radar screen, when the IFF button was pressed on the panel on the radar set. We learned how to construct grids on maps and how to read map locations down to a tenth of a mile, drawing grids in our exercise books. I found it extremely interesting.

On one of the days, we were taken by lorry to the end of the airfield landing strip, where a blue and white chequered van was standing, in the van's roof was an 'astrodome' and inside the van were a couple of erks, looking at a radar screen. A thick black cable ran from the back of the van to a long thin radar mast, which was busily nodding up and down looking right back up the runway. The airmen were reading off heights of incoming aircraft as they approached the airfield's runway. It was a beautiful day and, as we were only able to go into the van in twos and threes, the waiting time was spent laying on the grass in the November sunshine, it seemed a long way from West Kirby and those shouting drill instructors.

The second week, we paraded on the Monday morning and found a coach awaiting us on the parade ground. The corporal checked us all on board and the vehicle drove off out of the main gate, turning left in the direction of Stockbridge. About 2 miles along the road, we came to the small village of Nether Wallop where we turned right at the crossroads. About another ¾ of a mile along that road passing thatched cottages and watercress beds, the coach turned right through some large gateposts and we caught sight of a very large house, not quite a stately home, but a very grand building. This was where the remainder of our training was to take place.

Some of the large rooms had been converted into Operations plotting rooms, with large maps of the southern part of England displayed. The maps were marked out with lettered and numbered graphs and it was here that we were taught how to plot aircraft movements. The practice was quite realistic, we learned how to pick up identity plaques with the plotting roads, a trigger in the handle operating a grip at the end of the plotting rod, the other side of the rod had a magnetic head, which was activated by a second trigger. Placing the flat metal head onto the arrow and pressing the trigger, magnetised the head and allowed us to pick up one of the metal arrows. The plaques had three slide positions on them, into which were put the identity letters, 'F' for fighter, 'H' for hostile and 'X' for unidentified. The letter was followed by a number, to indicate individual plots, for example F135, (Fighter 135). The number stayed with the plot throughout the time the aircraft was flying through the sector controlling the flight, and on into the next sector until the aircraft landed. The second slide down the plaque showed number of aircraft, which was normally 1, but in our practice plots often showed wartime type plots of large numbers of attacking aircraft and could be displayed as, for example, 20+. The third and bottom slide showed the height at which the aircraft was flying, i.e. the figures 18 indicated that the aircraft was flying at eighteen thousand feet. A plaque was prepared by a 'raid orderly', on instruction from the plotter, who, on receiving the information through his headset, from the filter control centre (known as CFP – Central Filtered Plotting), would shout out the instructions to the 'raid orderly'. An example might be, 'Hostile 186, 15+ at angels 23' the raid orderly would the prepare a plaque as follows:-

H186

15+

23

Whilst the plaque was being prepared, the plotter would place a coloured arrow on the map grid reference, read out by the teller from the CFP. The colour of the arrow used was determined by the time the plot was received. At the head of the sloping plotting table was a set of three coloured lights, RED, YELLOW and BLUE. The lights were synchronised with a clock on the wall, known as a 'colour change clock'. Each five-minute segment of the clock was marked out by a coloured pyramid, with the apex of the pyramid facing in to the centre of the clock. Whilst the minute finger was traversing the 'red' segment, the synchronised red light would be lit up. Immediately the minute finger moved into the 'yellow' segment, the yellow light would come on and the red light would go out. By looking at the arrows plotted on the map, the aircraft controller could tell how old a plot was and how fast an aircraft was travelling. Each day we became more proficient at plotting and using our equipment, there was less dropping of plaques and fumbling with the plotting rods. As we progressed, the information coming though the headphones was speeded up until we were at a stage where we could take our proficiency test. We learned phonetic alphabet, practising each night from the notes in our exercise books. Later in my service I had to re-learn the phonetic alphabet, when the RAF adopted the NATO system, which brought the entire member air forces up to the same standard. I still get the two mixed up from time to time, 'Alpha with Able', 'Bravo with Baker' 'Delta with Dog' and so on, it got most complicated. We were obliged to learn the filter plotting side of the trade, although, being posted to a Sector Operations Centre, I was never to use that part of my training, just as my colleagues at the CFP never used their Operations table plotting skills, once at their permanent posting.

And so the time passed at RAF Middle Wallop.

About half way through the course, we were given a 48-hour pass. When I became aware of the fact that the pass was due, I asked my friend Levy how difficult it was to get home to Sheffield from Middle Wallop. I had no idea of the distances involved. Levy said that he was going home that weekend and said that he would be 'thumbing' it, which is hitchhiking. He said I could accompany him on the journey. He told me the return journey was by train to Birmingham, where he always joined a coach that ran weekly between Birmingham and the camp. There were many 'Brummies' on the camp, both airmen and soldiers, as, at that time, the camp was shared by both sections of the armed services.

I can't recall exactly where we started 'thumbing' it, but I can remember us arriving at a roadside café on the A1 (Great North

Road, as it was called then). Outside the café was a large vehicle park and the café was well patronised by both car and lorry drivers. We went into the café, which was noisy but warm. We bought some food and a drink and sat at a table already occupied by a young squaddie (soldier). We struck up a conversation with the squaddie and he asked if we were thumbing it, and where were we going. We told him we were both heading for Sheffield. He asked if we were taking lifts with any type of vehicle. Levy said we were trying to get lifts with cars because they were faster, but that we would accept any reasonable lift. The squaddie said he was heading for North Yorkshire and he was accepting any kind of vehicle, so long as it took him in the direction of home. He finished his mug of tea, wished us good luck and left the café. We watched him walk across the vehicle-park and disappear from view.

When we had finished our refreshment, we went to the toilet and then out onto the Vehicle Park. We walked along the edge of the road, glancing over our shoulder at the on-coming traffic and waving our thumbs at the passing traffic. We had only gone a short distance when two brand new Vauxhall cars came into view; both cars had red and white trade plates on the front, held onto the front bumper by thick black rubber bands. We waved our extended thumbs at the drivers and the first car braked heavily, the second car pulling in behind it. We ran to the first car and opened the front passenger door. 'Where are you going lads?' asked the driver. We replied in unison, 'Sheffield'. 'We're not supposed to carry passengers, but if one of you wants to get in this car and the other in my mates car at the back, we can take you as far as Doncaster'. We couldn't believe our luck. Levy went to the second car and I got into the first and off we went northwards. We must have been north of Luton, as the cars were fresh from the Vauxhall factory and on delivery, this was before the days of the massive car transporters, cars in those days were delivered either by rail, or individually. I remember we made one stop on the way to Doncaster. At that stop the car drivers bought us some refreshments. The funniest thing, however, was that about a mile after being picked up we passed a lorry; sitting up on top of the load, hanging on to a rope, was our squaddie friend. He certainly was taking any lift he could. We had a comfortable journey through to Doncaster.

Before the Doncaster by-pass was constructed, the A1 ran through the centre of the town. As can be imagined the traffic in the centre of Doncaster was a nightmare, as it was in many of the small towns and villages through which the road ran. Stilton, Stamford, Grantham, etc. all suffered from the heavy traffic in the days before the A1M and the building of bypasses.

We were dropped in the centre of Doncaster. It was dark and I was tired and totally lost, but Levy knew the town centre and we walked on until he said, 'This is the road that leads to Sheffield'. We turned left and started walking along the road; there was not much traffic. I had looked at my watch when we got out of the Vauxhall car and had noted the time was a quarter to midnight. I was pessimistic about our chances of getting a lift for the final leg of our journey and was feeling a bit dejected. Suddenly we saw headlamps approaching and Levy started waving his thumb madly. The car, which was travelling very fast, hurtled past us but screeched to a stop about fifty yards in front of us. We ran towards it and the rear passenger door opened. A man in evening dress, complete with black dickey-bow tie, leaned out of the door.

'Where are you going lads?' he shouted, adding, 'We're headed for Sheffield.' Once again fate had smiled on us. The car was a chauffeur-driven Daimler limousine and when we said we were going to Sheffield, the man invited us into the back of the car.

There was a partition separating the front and rear of the car and two small seats pulled down from the back of the partition. The man motioned us towards the seats. On the offside of the rear bench seat was a woman clad in a long evening dress and wearing a white fur stole around her neck. I noticed the man had a blue ribbon slung round his neck with some sort of medal attached to it. The man said, 'Will the Town Hall in Sheffield be a suitable place to drop you'? We said 'Yes, thank you' in unison. The man motioned to his chauffeur and we sped off into the night. The couple were very interested in where we stationed and how far we had travelled. In no time at all we pulled up outside the Sheffield Town Hall and as we alighted, we thanked the man and woman for helping us complete our journey home. It was about ten past midnight, the car had travelled the eighteen miles between Doncaster and Sheffield in less than half an hour. I have often wondered who the man was; he was obviously somebody important.

We only had a few yards to walk to the tram shelter at the side of the Peace Gardens. The tram service in Sheffield ran through the night and, at about twenty past twelve trams started to arrive at the stop. I boarded the tram bound for Meadowhead, which passed through Heeley, whilst Levy boarded the car for Ecclesall. We had arranged to meet at the Midland Station at 8 o'clock on Sunday to catch the train for Birmingham, where we would meet up with the coach bound for RAF Middle Wallop.

I arrived home tired from the long journey. Even though it was late, I spent some time talking to my Mum and Dad, before retiring to the comfort of my own bed. The following day, Saturday, I slept in late.

In the afternoon I went to the home of my friend, Michael Staniland. I had two friends with the same name, Michael, so Mick Staniland was always referred to as 'Stan', by the group I mixed with. Stan's dad was a bus driver, whilst my father also worked for the Corporation Transport Department, Dad was a bus conductor. I had met Stan at secondary school, we had both passed the 'eleven-plus' and had gone to Carfield Secondary School. My other friend Mick Dickinson, went to another school, I had been a friend of Mick 'Dick', (as he was referred to), since the age of five.

On arrival at Stan's home, his mum and young sister Dianne greeted me. Everything seemed all right and I was busy telling them of my adventures over the preceding weeks, when suddenly Mrs Staniland burst in to tears. I was very embarrassed and did not know what was wrong, until Mrs Staniland went over to the sideboard. She opened a drawer and took out a piece of paper and passed it to me.

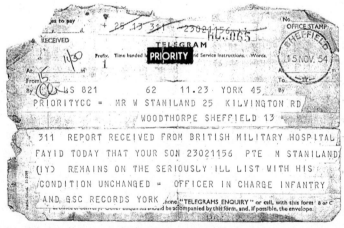

The paper was a telegram from the Ministry of Defence and advised Mr and Mrs Staniland that their son, Michael, had been seriously injured in a road accident, whilst serving with the army in Egypt. Mrs Staniland told me that Stan was in the military hospital at Wheatley, near Oxford. The news really put the 'mockers' on my weekend. Mrs Staniland asked if I would be able to go and visit Stan. I said I would try as hard as I could to get permission to go and see him. She gave me the telegram to take with me to show my superiors at RAF Middle Wallop. I promised to write and tell her whether I had been able to visit him. I stayed at the Staniland's for about another hour and then took my leave, going home and then went to meet Mick Dick. That night we went to the cinema, our usual activity.

Sunday morning was another luxurious lay-in and I got up just in time to have my Sunday lunch, which in our house was always a roast, with potatoes, vegetables, Yorkshire puddings, and gravy. When you had eaten one of Mum's meals, all you felt like doing was sleeping. I spent the afternoon watching television and before I knew it Mum was asking whether it was time for me to get ready to go back. I had a wash and got all of my things together, packing them in my backpack, which I had brought with me. Mum had packed me some 'goodies' up, some for the return journey and a larger amount for me to eat when I got back to camp.

When the time came, I reluctantly took leave of my family and made my way down to the Midland Station. In the last couple of months I had been on more trains than ever before in my life. At the station I met Levy as planned, I felt very secure to have him to guide me on my journey. We caught the Birmingham train and, on arrival in that big city, I followed Levy to the place from where the coach departed to RAF Middle Wallop. It was my first visit to Birmingham, but I saw very little of the place. The coach was fairly full of both airmen and soldiers. Middle Wallop was the home of the Army Air Corps and there was a large contingent of army personnel based there at the time of my stay. (Middle Wallop eventually became 100%

army and continues that way today, being the base for helicopter training for army pilots).

The journey was made in the dark all the way and, apart from the small towns and villages we passed through, I saw little of the countryside through which we passed. Most people on the coach seemed to be asleep, but I couldn't sleep and spent most of the time watching the silhouettes of trees and bushes and the occasional house rush by the coach window. After what seemed an age the coach pulled into the gates of RAF Middle Wallop, where its load of weary servicemen alighted, walking in hushed groups towards the 'H' blocks and other billets.

The next morning it was back to the routine, 'up like the lark', ablutions, and off to breakfast. Back to the 'H' block to dump our irons and then pick up our notebooks and pencils and then off to catch the transport down to the training centre.

I waited until NAAFI break before asking the Sergeant if I could see someone about arranging a visit to see Stan in the military hospital. I still didn't know whether I would be allowed any time off, or whether I would have to wait until the weekend. The Sergeant took me before the training unit's commanding officer. I explained why I had asked to see him and handed over the telegram, given to me by Mrs. Staniland. The commanding officer read the telegram and then asked when I would like to visit my friend, I said as soon as possible if it was convenient. The officer said he would allow me a one-day compassionate leave pass and said I could take the following day away from my training schedule, he then issued me with a one-day pass. I expressed my thanks and he excused me, I saluted, leaving the office to return to my trade training.

The next day, after breakfast, and resplendent in my best blue, greatcoat, gloves and peaked cap, I left the main gate and stood at the bus stop for Andover. I had discussed my route with some of the lads and was informed that I would have to travel from Andover to Newbury and then on to Oxford, each journey being made by bus. On reaching Oxford I would have to catch a further bus to the Military Hospital at Wheatley. The journey took most of the morning. I had taken some of my Mum's goodies with me for sustenance on the journey. On arrival at the hospital gates, I found I had to walk up a long drive to the hospital. I went into the reception and asked if I could see Private Michael Staniland. I was told to wait; eventually a young nurse came up to me and asked if I was the visitor for Michael Staniland. I nodded and she led me along some corridors and eventually into a ward, with beds lining either side. We walked about three-quarters the way down the ward, past beds in which young men lay, some looking worse than others. We stopped at one of the beds and there was my mate, his hair was dishevelled and his eyes had a glassy stare. The nurse said loudly, ' Your friend has come to see you Michael'. Stan just looked at me with a blank look on his face, he seemed not to know me. I spent about one hour sat at the side of the bed, trying to make conversation, but getting very little response. I asked Stan how he had been injured, but was as wise when I left the hospital, as I had been when I went in. My friend was not a well person and I felt uncomfortable. It was a new experience for me, hospital visiting, and I felt somewhat helpless, seeing my friend in such a condition. Looking at my watch I told Stan I would have to go and said I hoped to see him when he got home. He gave me a blank look and I left the ward, looking back at him as I reached the door. He was just sat there, propped up with pillows, staring at the opposite wall.

I left the hospital building and walked down the long drive. On reaching the main road, I looked left and saw a bus displaying 'Oxford' on its destination blind. From the speed of the bus, I knew I would not be able to get across the road in time to reach the bus stop. I waved frantically at the bus driver but he either did not see me, or he ignored me. Missing that bus started, what was to be, the most traumatic 24 hours of my young life.

Crossing the road, I walked down to the bus stop and examined the timetable, which was displayed on the side of the shelter. The next bus would be in one hour. I knew the direction from which I had come and so started walking in towards the city of Oxford. I walked near to the edge of the road and kept waving my right, extended thumb, at the traffic coming down the road. I must have walked for about a quarter of a mile, when suddenly a RAF lorry came into sight. I waved my thumb and was delighted when the lorry pulled up. I opened the passenger door and the driver, in working blue with a sleeveless leather jacket over his blouse-jacket, said, 'Where are you going, Oxford?', I replied, 'Yes', 'Jump in', he said. I climbed into the cab of the lorry. It was a small Ford lorry with a snub nose of wartime vintage and the cab was very sparse. The driver was a friendly sort and chatted merrily all the way into Oxford. He asked where I was stationed and what I was doing in that part of the country. I explained my mission to see my injured friend and said I was on compassionate leave. I can't remember where he was from or where he was going, but I was certainly thankful for the lift, it was cold and the light was fading. I was in strange territory and miles away from Middle Wallop. My RAF friend dropped me right in the bus station at Oxford, wished me 'all the best' and drove off. I walked into the bus station to find that I had just missed the bus to Newbury, again there was an hour to wait for the next bus. I had a walk round looking in the shops. Near the bus station was a large Leyland lorry and trailer. In large letters along the side of the vehicle was the legend, 'MOBILE X-RAY UNIT'.

~ In Defence of the Realm ~

Members of the general public were entering the vehicle and there were some young nurses speaking to people, encouraging them to have a chest x-ray. For the want of something to do, I entered the lorry and had a chest x-ray. Apparently I was all right and had no problems with my lungs. After leaving the mobile x-ray unit, I looked at my watch and realised I would have to hurry to catch my bus. Luckily the bus was still in and I boarded the vehicle paying through to Newbury. It was now well dark and the journey between Oxford and Newbury was somewhat boring. I sat on the top deck of the bus trying to peer out into the dark countryside. Just after 8pm, the bus pulled into Newbury bus station. I alighted and caught sight of an Inspector. I went up to the Inspector and asked where I would catch the bus to Andover and what time would it leave. The Inspector told me that the last bus to Andover had departed and that there would not be another bus until 8.30am the next day. I was mortified. Coming from a large city, where the transport system operated through the night, the last thing I expected was that I would not be able to catch a bus, at what I considered, was early evening. For a few moments I was stunned. I asked the Inspector which direction I would have to go to get to Andover.

He took me out of the bus station and pointed me in the right direction and I started to walk. I was scared stiff. I hadn't a clue what to do other than to start hitchhiking again. I started walking down the road, what little traffic there was ignored my thumb. Then, to make matters worse, it started to snow, big floating flakes, which quickly covered my shoulders and the front of my greatcoat. I was really depressed by this time and feeling that, 'somebody up there doesn't like me'. I could see the end of the road lights and the pavement disappearing where the houses finished. I decided to stop walking and just stand at the side of the road. I was really 'brassed off'.

Suddenly, out of the misty snowflakes, a pair of headlights appeared. It was a large lorry, its windscreen wipers making heavy work of clearing a portion of each screen. The lorry passed me and then cam to a stop, I slithered my way to the passenger door and opened it, the door was very heavy. From inside the dark interior of the cab, a friendly voice shouted over the engine noise, 'Where y'going son?'. I shouted back, 'Andover'. 'Jump in', said the voice. Elated, I climbed up into the lorry and slammed the door. The driver clunked the vehicle into gear and the lorry struggled away from the side of the road. 'I'm not exactly going to Andover', said the driver, 'But I'm going so far, I'll drop you off where this road crosses the Andover road.

It was nice and warm in the lorry, the engine being in between the two seats, helped warm the vehicle, but was very noisy. The driver and I carried out a shouted conversation as we chugged along the snow-covered highway. For a short time I felt a bit more comfortable. The driver had to keep leaning forward and wiping the condensation from the window as, on the outside, the windscreen wipers struggled to keep the centre of each window clear. After some time we arrived at a straight crossroads, there were trees on every side of the junction. The driver stopped the lorry and pointed to the right. 'That's the Andover road', he said. It was pitch black and we had not seen any other vehicles for ages. I quickly weighed up the situation, if I got out here, I felt I would soon be in serious trouble. It was still snowing heavily and I had no idea where I was. If I alighted there I feared I would be found in a snowdrift, frozen to death.

I shouted to the driver, 'What's the next town you will come to?',

'Winchester', he replied.

'If you don't mind, I'll stay with you until we reach there', I said.

'That's fine with me young man', said the driver. He put the vehicle into gear and we set off again.

We eventually reached Winchester, which was in darkness. At that time it was still the general practice to switch off all the street lights after a certain time, in most towns and cities. The driver stopped the lorry, saying this was the city centre. I thanked him for the lift and climbed down from the lorry. It was not snowing in Winchester, although the roads were wet.

I stood there for a short time wondering what to do, I was frightened. In the distance I could see a light and so I thought, where there is a light there could be people, so I made my way towards the light. For once I was in luck, when I got to the light I saw it was illuminating a signboard which proclaimed, 'Hampshire Regiment'. To the right of the board was a guardroom. I went to the guardroom door and went in, there was an army corporal sat at a desk. The corporal looked up on hearing the door open and said, 'Can I help you?' I explained my predicament and the corporal suggested that I go to the local police station, saying that he would show me the way.

We went out into the cold night and the corporal pointed down the road, explaining the location of the police station. I thanked him and followed his directions through the dark streets. Eventually I saw the blue lamp hanging outside a building, with the word POLICE on each side of the lamp in white letters. I went into the police station and up to the counter, which stretched the full length of the room.

A police sergeant was seated at a desk. He got up and came to the counter, saying, 'What can I do for you son?' Once again I went through my tale of woe, explaining that I was totally lost. The sergeant said that the best thing he could do was to telephone through to RAF Middle Wallop and see whether they would provide some transport for me. He asked my name and then picked up the telephone, asking the telephone operator for RAF Middle Wallop, he then replaced the telephone into its cradle.

After a few minutes the telephone bell gave a piercing ring and the sergeant picked up the phone once more. I heard him say, 'This is the police at Winchester, we have a young airman named Voyse who appears to have lost his way, are you able to provide transport for him back to Middle Wallop?'. The sergeant then went quiet, obviously listening to the person at the other end. He then said, 'Oh all right, I'll tell him, thank you'. He put the telephone down. He looked at me seriously and said, 'I'm sorry son, they only provide transport for WAAFS', (members of the Women's Royal Air Force, or WRAF). 'You can stay here for the night if you like and catch the first bus to Andover', he continued. I must have looked a sorry sight, for he followed by saying, 'Would you like a cup of tea son?' I replied, 'Yes please!' Pointing in the direction of a long seat he said, 'Sit over there young man, I'll make you a pot of tea'. I sat down feeling sorry for myself, it looked like being a long night. After a short while, the sergeant came back to the counter, lifted up the end of the counter and came over to me, he had a pot of tea in one hand and a plate with some sandwiches in the other. 'I suppose you're hungry as well' he said, I nodded. (I have often wondered since where he got the sandwiches from, and whether they were from his own packing up.) The food was welcome; it seemed ages since I had last eaten. Whilst I was eating the sandwiches the sergeant was talking to me, he asked how long I had been in the air force and what part of the country I came from. When I said I was from Sheffield, he said, 'I thought that was a Yorkshire accent'.

When I had finished eating the sergeant said, 'I can't offer you a proper bed, but you can get your head down on one of the so called beds in the cells, follow me'. I followed him through to the other side of the counter and he led me to a cell, which led off from the office. 'Get your head down there son,' he said, 'If any of our cars come in, I'll see if I can get them to run you over to Middle Wallop'. The sergeant had not let me down so far, so I was fairly optimistic that he would try his best to help me. I took my greatcoat off and turning it inside out, I folded it into a pillow. I lay on the hard wooden 'bed', put my head on my makeshift pillow and after some time drifted into a fitful sleep. The lift did not materialise. Sometime during the night I woke up and could hear the sound of someone crying, I could hear a male voice saying, 'The accident happened near Basingstoke, we've arranged for a car to take you to Basingstoke hospital'. What had happened I never found out, but someone had obviously got worse problems than I had.

It was still dark when I was shaken awake by the sergeant, 'If you want to catch that first bus, you better get up', then, handing me a pot of tea, he said, 'get that down you young man'. I drank the tea, sitting on the 'bed' and, after finishing it, shook my overcoat out and put it on, the coat was still damp from the snow and badly creased. I made my way out of the cell and through the office and to the other side of the counter. I asked the sergeant where the bus station was located. 'Just a minute son' he said, 'I'll come and show you'. He came from behind the counter and took me to the door, it was very cold outside. He pointed me in the direction of the bus station and said, 'Good luck young man'. I replied by thanking him for the tea, etc. and then went in the direction he had shown me. I found the bus station all right and located the Andover bus. I sat in the lower saloon of the bus, feeling very scruffy, I felt as though the other passengers were looking at me, I had not had a wash since the previous morning and, although I didn't have much of a beard, I still felt untidy.

The bus seemed to take ages to get to Andover, it must have called at all the villages in the area. As it came light I was able to see some of the passing countryside, last night's snow had gone, but it was still cold. I was very tired and kept nodding off. Eventually, the bus arrived at Andover where I transferred to a bus for Middle Wallop. As the bus approached the RAF station, I was filled with trepidation, I wondered what sort of trouble I would find myself in when I got there. The bus pulled up just before the camp entrance and I alighted. I walked down towards the guardroom, to where 'scarface' the RAF policeman was standing, resplendent in his 'whites'. As I approached he looked sternly at me and said, 'Airman Voyse?' 'Yes corporal', I meekly replied. His next words filled me with dread, 'We've been waiting for you', he said, I thought, 'Things can't get any worse'. 'Get down to your training unit and report to Sergeant Brown'. My heart was pounding in my chest as I went back out of the camp and turned left towards Nether Wallop. If I had known, I could have stayed on the bus. The training unit was about three miles from RAF Middle Wallop, not a long way in the transport vehicles, but in my tired condition, it seemed to take me ages to get there. I had not had any food since having the sandwiches in the police station, I was tired and full of dread. When I reached Nether Wallop, I had to turn right and follow that road for a while to get to the big house where the training unit was located.

I eventually arrived and reported to the sergeant. 'The C.O. wants to see you', said the sergeant, 'Come with me'. He led me to the commanding officer's office and, on arriving at the door, said, 'Wait there'.

Boy, was I scared. Eventually the sergeant came out and said, 'Right Airman, in you go, left, right, left, right, mark time, HALT!!'. I stood to attention in front of the commanding officer, I was by this time close to tears. The C.O. then laid into me, telling me that I was ungrateful, I had let him down, and thrown his generosity in his face. He generally railed me for being back late from the compassionate leave. He asked me for an explanation, and, as I told him what had happened to me, I could feel my chin wobbling with emotion, I don't know how I stopped myself from breaking into tears.

What had happened was not really my fault, but I was made to feel like a criminal. After bending my ear for some time, the officer eventually closed the interview and the sergeant marched me out. The sergeant was fairly easy on me and I went back to my lectures, still hungry, tired and feeling scruffy and considering I had been badly treated. I had tried my best to get back to the camp but was thwarted by the weather and my lack of knowledge of the area.

During my stay at RAF Middle Wallop, a couple of other things occurred, of a more humorous nature.

Every morning and afternoon we had a tea break. A NAAFI van used to come down from the main camp and we queued up for a drink and a bun. You could buy some of the best jam doughnuts I have ever tasted, from the van. Whether it was because we always seemed to be permanently hungry, or because the doughnuts were well made, I do not know, anyway they were my favourites when having a tea break. At the other side of the perimeter fence, which surrounded the training unit, there were fields and trees. In one of the fields there were always a large number of cows and, as is the nature of the bovine family, the cows were very nosy.

As soon as the lads started queuing at the NAAFI van, the cows would come meandering down the field to where the fence separated the field from the training unit grounds. Airmen got into the habit of pulling tufts of grass from their side of the fence and pushing it through the fence. As the old saying goes, 'the grass is always greener on the other side of the fence' and the cows made that saying a reality by jostling for the grass being pushed through the fence. Whether the farmer saw the airmen feeding his cows and complained, or one of the officers spotted us through the windows of the training unit I do not know. What did happen was that a notice went up on the perimeter fence one day, it read *'AIRMEN WILL NOT FRATERNISE WITH THE COWS',* it was signed by the commanding officer of the training unit.

Another funny incident occurred when we were involved in an exercise. We were told that the airfield was to be attacked by an enemy invasion force and that we would form a part of the defence force.

Army personnel and members of the RAF Regiment formed the invasion force. We were marched down to the armoury and queued up in alphabetical order to draw weapons. With a name beginning with 'V', I was right at the back of the queue, consequently, when I finally got into the armoury, they had run out of weapons. I was given a piece of paper on which was written, in handwriting, the word *'Rifle' (see below).*

Theoretically I should have handed the piece of paper in to the armoury, on the conclusion of the exercise, as instructed by the armourer who issued the chit; I did not, which is how I come to have it in my possession to this day.

I was somewhat disappointed at not having a weapon and when I went back to the barrack room later that day, I showed Levy what I was supposed to defend the airfield with. He told me he was not involved in the exercise and said that I could borrow his personal Lee Enfield 303 rifle. All permanent members of the station's personnel had their own rifle at Middle Wallop. Unlike at West Kirby, where the rifles were kept in racks in the middle of the room, at Middle Wallop, they had two hooks under the frame of the bed and the rifle was slung on the hooks. I never saw this system in operation at any of the other RAF stations I visited.

On the morning of the exercise and prior to its commencement, we were all issued with a clip of 'blank' ammunition. I loaded the clip into Levy's rifle and joined the others, awaiting instruction as to exactly what part of the airfield we were to defend. The morning was exceedingly misty and visibility was down to about two or three yards. We were taken to a part of the airfield and were instructed to lay our ground sheets (capes) on the floor and defend that area. When we laid down on our ground sheets, we were amazed that we could see under the layer of mist. It was a real weird sight to see legs, without bodies, walking around us. The exercise started and was mainly boring, the attacking forces were throwing 'thunder-flashes' about, which I considered highly dangerous because of the poor visibility. When the exercise was over, we saw a lad who had had a hole blown in his ground sheet by one of the thunder-flashes. At our part of the airfield we saw no action, but nevertheless, every so often, an airman (including myself) would let off a blank, just to liven up the proceedings. Any way I used up my full clip of blanks.

When the exercise was over and I returned to my room, I hung Levy's rifle on the hooks, under his bed and went for my evening meal. When I returned from the cookhouse, Levy had come in from work. He gave me a right 'roasting', saying, 'Have you seen the state of this rifle?' He slid open the bolt and held the rifle up in the air, looking up the spout. He then passed the rifle to me, I looked up the spout and I had to agree with him, the barrel of the rifle was absolutely filthy. I spent the rest of the evening stripping the rifle and cleaning it with the 'pull-through', which was kept in a small compartment in the butt of the rifle, some 4 x 2 and the foul smelling oil that was used for cleaning weapons.

One day, our corporal instructor asked if anyone would like to have a flight in an aeroplane. Most of us were keen. He told us that, if we went down to the hangars, early on any Saturday morning, and helped to push out the planes, we would have the opportunity to have a flight. The following Saturday, bright and early, a group of us made our way to one of the hangars, where, directed, by a flight-sergeant, we pushed out about eight aircraft. I can't remember what they were, but they were all two seaters fighters and had a bulbous cowling under the engine. The pilots eventually arrived and so did about half a dozen WAAFS. The upshot was that only a couple of our lads were lucky enough to have a flight, I was one of the disappointed ones. When our friends returned from the flight, one of them was full of how great it was and that he had seen the coast of France. The other lad was not so happy, apparently the pilot he had had decided to do some aerobatics, with the consequence that our friend had been as sick as a dog and had been obliged to clean out the rear cockpit on his return from the flight. According to him the pilot seemed to think it very amusing. I would only get one other opportunity to fly, whilst in the RAF.

Every Saturday night, a coach left the camp and went to Southampton. Levy asked me if I had ever seen a 'tit and leg' show, I told him that I had not had that dubious pleasure. Well one Saturday night, I paid my dues and joined a full coach of airmen, including some non-commissioned officers and off we went to Southampton. I don't know which route the driver took, but we went over seven humpback bridges (more of them later).

On arrival in Southampton, we walked in a noisy group to the Grand Theatre, where we climbed, what seemed like hundreds of steps, to the upper balcony (or 'Gods', as it was known). We were in the very top of the theatre and the angle of the balcony, on which we sat, was very steep. At the front of the balcony was a large brass handrail, presumably to stop anyone falling down into the 'circle' balcony, which jutted out below. The show consisted of various 'turns', which were interspersed with what were termed as 'tableaux'. After an artist, such as a comedian had been on the stage, performing in front of the large closed curtains, the lights on the stage dimmed and the curtains rose slowly. Scattered around the stage, at various levels, were a number of nude young ladies, with lengths of cloth draped over their private parts, but exposing at least one, or both breasts. The ladies stood perfectly still and looked just like statues. At that time the law forbade any moving nudes on both the stage and screen. Officials from the Lord Chamberlain's office made sure that the law was not being broken, by vetting films, plays and stage shows.

You can imagine the reaction of a large number of sex-starved airmen to the sight of bare female flesh, regardless of how little could be seen from the distance of the upper balcony. A large cheer went up and there were countless wolf-whistles. The ladies bravely held their poses for a number of minutes before the lights went down and the curtains closed. The following act, regardless of what it was, or how well it was performed, suffered catcalls and booing from the unruly crowd I found myself a member of. One act consisted of a girl with two enormous feathered fans, who to all intents and purpose was nude. She danced to the music played by the orchestra, ingeniously moving the fans across her body, showing bare shoulders and legs, but very little else. Again the crowd of erks encouraged her to reveal more.

We left the theatre at the end of the show and made our way to the place where the coach was to pick us up. Some of the lads had been drinking both, before the show, during the interval and on their way back to the coach. Others, who had not been to the theatre, must have spent the evening drinking. Believe it or not, at that time, I, at the age of eighteen, had only ever been in one public house, and that was in the village of West Kirby. Neither had I drunk much alcohol. My father had been a member of the Methodist church and we never had any alcoholic drinks at home. I can recall that my mother had once got tipsy after an outing with some friends and the sight of her not acting her normal self had both frightened me, as a young child, and confused me, I never saw her that way again ever. I was one of the few sober airmen returning to the coach. On the journey back to RAF Middle Wallop there were the same seven humpback bridges, which the coach driver went over at some speed. My stomach churned and I had not had any drink. You can imagine what the reaction to the bridges was from those under the influence of alcohol. People were throwing up all over the coach and the inside smelt awful and nearly made me sick. I was relieved when we finally arrived at the camp entrance. We descended from the coach under the gaze of two S.P.s, one of whom I recognised as 'scarface'. Miraculously even the very drunken airmen managed to regain enough control over their body movements whilst they ran the gauntlet of the guardroom and its keepers.

At last our trade training was finalised and we took the tests which were to qualify us as 'Fighter Plotter/Radar Operators'. Everyone was successful, that is with the exception of a corporal, who was trying to redraft himself into another trade. His specified trade was Administrative Orderly (the general dogs-bodies of the RAF), at the beginning of the course he had told us that, every so often, he tried to learn a new trade and so applied for various courses. So far he had not been successful. Once again our corporal friend had failed. Having come straight from square-bashing, we had treated him with some awe at first, but he was gradually treated by us as 'one of the lads', as we got to know him. He was what the Americans would have termed a 'sad sack'. I felt sorry for him when he told us he had failed, nonetheless he appeared quite cheerful about his failure and said, he would leave it a few months and try for something else. I often wondered if he had ever managed to succeed in getting transferred to another trade, before leaving the service.

The end of trade training was a repeat of the end of square-bashing, we had got to know each other quite well and had made friends. Suddenly, we were at the end of the course and we were given our postings to the permanent unit we were to join. I was to be split up from my friend from Stirling, seeing him only once more again, incredibly when changing trains at a railway station, when we were both crossing a footbridge in different directions, dashing to catch connecting trains. We were only able to exchange brief words, asking each other how we were getting on, and Jock went out of my life forever.

One airman from West Kirby, Chris from Dewsbury, received the same posting as me and we were destined to stay together throughout our service, although never becoming close friends.

My orders were to report to Royal Air Force Longley Lane and both Chris and I had rail warrants, which allowed us to travel between Andover and Preston in Lancashire. We were provided with a packed lunch, taken in the back of a '3-tonner' RAF transport lorry to the station at Andover, where a gang of us joined the train for London. In the company of others I felt quite confident.

In London Chris and I joined a northbound train for a journey to Lancashire, up the West Coast line of British Railways. The journey seemed to take forever. At last we arrived at Preston station, where, laden down heavily with our full kit, we left the train. We made our way out of the station asking the ticket collector if he could direct us to RAF Longley Lane. The ticket collector said he was unable to help us, he said the only RAF stations near to Preston were Weeton, Kirkham and Warton, he advised us to ask a taxi driver in the taxi rank outside the station.

We went up to one of the taxis and asked for directions, again the person being asked gave us a puzzled look, he said he had never heard of RAF Longley Lane. He suggested we try the Ribble bus station and pointed us in the right direction. We had had a long day and were tired and hungry, we walked through the town centre of Preston and found the bus station, where we went to the enquiry office, asking again for RAF Longley Lane. Again puzzled looks from the bus inspector. Both of us were now very worried, we thought we had been given wrong instructions and wondered what we should do next. Suddenly a bus crew came into the office. The inspector said, 'Have either of you two heard of RAF Longley Lane?'. The bus driver shook his head, but the conductress said, 'There's something to do with the RAF up near Goosnargh on our route, I wonder if that's what you want?'. By this time, we were not only tired and hungry, but also fed up and ready for a sit down. We followed the bus crew to their vehicle and boarded, sitting in the lower saloon, across from where the conductress was seated. The vehicle moved off and we travelled through the centre of Preston and out onto the A6, we were soon out into the country and before long travelling along narrow country lanes. Eventually the conductress announced, 'this is about it' pressing the bell for the driver to stop. We alighted from the bus into complete darkness. In the fields at the other side of a hedge we could see the outline, of what appeared to be huts. It seemed strange that there was a large distance between each hut. We stumbled along and Chris suddenly said, 'Look!' I looked and saw in the dim light a large board on which was painted, 'RAF POLICE DOGS PATROL THIS AREA'. We had obviously arrived at something to do with the RAF, but what?

5. RAF Longley Lane (1)

(Where I become a mole)

Whilst trying to determine where exactly we were, we heard the now familiar whining of a Bedford engine, coming from the direction of the route we had travelled. We turned and saw headlamps approaching us. The vehicle was a wartime utility coach and on picking us out in his headlights, the driver stopped the coach. We went to the door, which someone pulled open from inside. A voice shouted, 'Are you looking for Longley Lane?', before we had a chance to answer, the driver, who was leaning back looking towards the door, shouted, 'Jump on'. We struggled on board with all of our possessions. On board the coach besides the driver, were two airmen and a RAF policeman.

The policeman was holding a leather strap to which was fastened an Alsatian dog. The dog was completely blocking the aisle of the coach. The coach moved off and after a short distance made a right turn, travelling about a hundred yards before coming to a stop again. The driver said, 'Leave your stuff on one of the seats and come with us'. We followed the driver off the coach and out into the night once more. We were walking on a cinder-covered surface and to the right I could make out what appeared to be a small hillock. The two airmen, who were both carrying rolled up blankets, followed us. The policeman followed at the rear with his dog. We reached a paved path and walked by some bushes to where there appeared a lit up entrance, which seemed to disappear into the side of the hillock. I was totally puzzled. The driver led the way down four steps and then through a large door into a sort of concrete lined porch. To the right was another large door, which he opened and we followed him into a small corridor about 15 feet long, at the end of which was another door. We went through the final door and found ourselves inside an underground bunker. Immediately to the left was a counter, behind which was seated a RAF policeman. 'Two sprogs, just been posted', said the driver, nodding in the direction of me and Chris, 'We found them wandering about outside'. The policeman asked us for our details and then told us that we would be taken to RAF Warton, when the coach left later. To one of the airmen he said, 'Make them a pot of tea Smithy'. The airman said, 'Follow me lads', and, turning right, he started down a staircase. We followed going deeper into the bunker. I was still confused as to what was happening and where we were.

The airman made us a drink and we sat in a small office. 'This is where you'll work', said the airman, 'We're on fire-piquet and so we'll be here all night, the coach will take you back to the domestic site at Warton, when the driver is ready'. While he was talking, the policeman with the dog was rolling a brass tin down the corridor. The tin had the legend '8 sausages' on the side. Each time he rolled the tin, his dog ran down the corridor, its back legs skidding on the polished floor. The dog grabbed the tin and ran back to the policeman, dropping the tin at the policeman's feet and, with its head right down on its front paws, wagged its tail violently, awaiting the next throw. By the time it had finished, the tin was full of dents.

Eventually Smithy came into the small office saying, 'Right lads, the coach is going back to Warton. You had better get back upstairs before he leaves without you'. I was still confused as to what was happening and as to where Warton was. We went back up the stairs to the police desk. The coach driver was leaning on the counter speaking to the RAF policeman. 'Follow me', he said, starting off through the big steel doors into the small corridor, which led to the outer doors. We followed and eventually arrived back at the coach. The driver jumped into the driving seat and started up the engine, 'Make yourselves comfortable lads, its about thirteen miles to RAF Warton'. He then put the vehicle in gear and drove across the cinder-covered car park, turning left out onto the country road. We could see nothing out of the side windows and very little in the dim headlights to the front. After about a mile we came to a main road and could see a small public house all lit up across the other side of the main road. At the junction the coach driver turned left and we started off down, what I later learned, was a part of the A6. There was more traffic on this road and, on passing a sign, I read that we were heading towards Preston.

The coach proceeded on through Preston, and out of the other side of the town, in the direction of Blackpool. Eventually I saw a road sign that pointed to the left reading 'Lytham'. We carried on down the road passing through the village of Freckleton. I then saw a sign which read, 'Royal Air Force Warton', under the sign was painted, 'No. 2 Site'. During the journey the driver had told us that we would be staying on number 8 site, which was a 'domestic' site.

We passed a large entrance gate, which announced that it was 'No 1 site', I could see the well-illuminated guardroom and a RAF policeman standing at the door. On the left-hand side we passed the 'Astra' cinema, an establishment I was to get to know very well. After what seemed an age the coach started to slow down and the driver turned right into an entrance gate, the sign at the gate read 'Royal Air Force' in curved lettering pointing downwards at each end, there was a RAF roundel in the centre and the upward curved 'Warton', under which in a straight line it announced 'No. 8 Site'.

Immediately to our front, as we pulled into the gate, was a stanchion pole, in the down position. The driver said, 'Get your stuff lads and report to the guardroom, they'll tell you which hut you are in'. As we collected our gear and started to leave the coach, a RAF policeman came out and lifted the stanchion pole. We climbed off the coach and the driver drove forward, pipping his horn as he went past the policeman. The policeman raised his arm in a wave.

The policeman then lowered the stanchion pole and turned his attention to us, 'Are you Longley Lane wallers?', he asked, we both replied 'Yes corporal', in unison. 'Just a minute', said the policeman. We stood there waiting. Eventually he came back outside with a clipboard and read out our names. 'If you hang on there, someone will come and take you to your hut'. We waited again and eventually another RAF policeman came out of the guardroom and saying, 'Follow me', turned into the camp road and set off at a brisk pace.

By the time we had picked up our kit, he was well in front of us and we had to rush to catch him up. We passed the station flagpole to our right, went on up the road to where another road crossed, turned left. 'That's the cookhouse', shouted the policeman, pointing to the right, and shortly after, pointing to the left, he said, 'That's the NAAFI'. We then turned right into another road. There was lighting on the roads, but it was not very bright. On the left side of the road we could see there were brick built huts, whilst on the right hand side, was a line of Nissen huts, the curved shapes silhouetted against the night sky. Lights were shining from the huts on the left, but the Nissen huts were in complete darkness. Eventually, three-quarters of the way up the road, the policeman pointed, 'That's your billet, 148'. He turned across the grass towards one of the huts. Painted on the left-hand side of the door, on a white marked out square was the number, 148. This was to be my home for the rest of my service.

We followed the policeman into the hut, through a short corridor, with a door on either side, and then through an inner door into the hut proper. There were signs of habitation, towels hung over locker doors, made beds, caps on top of lockers, etc. but the hut was devoid of life. There were two unmade beds, both had piles of blankets at the foot and to the side of the blankets, neatly folded, were a couple of white sheets and two white pillowcases. To the left-hand side of each bed, stood a small locker and on its left, a tall locker; both lockers were open and empty.

'Take your pick', said the policeman, pointing in the direction of the first empty bed, then without saying anything else, he turned on his heel and left the hut. Being in front of Chris, I threw my kit bag onto the first empty bed, whilst Chris went about four beds further down and sat on his bed.

I took my greatcoat off and hung it in the large locker and immediately started to unpack my gear, stowing some items in each locker, my spare underclothes went into the small locker, whilst my 'working-blue' was hung in the large locker. Chris shouted, 'I wonder if we can get any grub in the cookhouse?'

I replied, 'I don't know, but perhaps we can get something in the NAAFI'. We carried on with our unpacking, as we spoke to one another. Suddenly the hut door opened and an airman with two inverted stripes, (corporal technician) walked in. Seeing the stripes, I shouted, 'NCO present' and stood to attention, Chris jumped up from his bed, standing rigidly to attention. The corporal said, 'Come on lads, there's no need for that here, you're not at square-bashing now, calm down'. We both relaxed somewhat, it was not easy to get out of the habit which had been instilled into us during our eight weeks at West Kirby. The corporal went through the usual, 'Where are you from?', 'What did you do in civvie-street?' questions. Then, after a short time, he said, 'Do you like listening to music?' Being still a bit on edge, I said, 'Yes corporal'. The corporal then suggested that, if we went to his room, we could listen to some music. Reluctantly, Chris and I followed the corporal to his room, which was through one of the side doors in the small corridor. We went into the small room, there was the bed, and lockers the same as we had, but he had the luxury of some bookshelves and a leather armchair. On the top of his small locker was a record player. 'Sit down' said the corporal, 'My name's Rex, by the way'. Chris having entered the room before me sat in the armchair; I sat on the edge of the bed. The corporal took a record out of its sleeve and placed it on the record player. 'You'll like this', he said. The music, which started playing, was a tune that I would remember for the rest of my life. When I heard it in future years, it brought back to me that first evening at RAF Warton.

In those times, we were mostly innocent youths, I for one had never heard about homosexuals. When I was very young, I remember my Dad giving us a talk, in a very embarrassed manner, about some people who he described as 'bum-boys', saying we should never associate with such people. It was all double-Dutch to me; I must have been about 8 years old at the time.

Anyhow, the record playing was by Stan Kenton and was (I found out later) titled 'Peanut Vendor'. As the music started to play the corporal sat next to me on the bed. Suddenly and without warning, the corporal started stroking the top of my right leg...

I looked at Chris in a panic. Chris said, 'Hadn't we better go and get some grub?' Thankfully, I said, 'Yes, I'm starving', and then to the corporal, 'We've had hardly anything to eat today'.

We both stood up and made our excuses and backed out of the corporal's room.

We were later to find out that the corporal was known as 'Sexy Rexy' by all and sundry at the camp, and he regularly pestered new arrivals at RAF Warton.

Chris and I made our way down to the NAAFI, where, having had a meal, we watched television for a while and then made our way back to the hut. When we arrived back in the hut there were a number of people there. The airmen introduced themselves and we were made to feel at home, neither of us mentioned the episode with the corporal technician. One of the lads advised me of the procedures the following morning. Apparently, after breakfast we were to parade outside our huts and would be marched down to the MT (Motor Transport) yard, from where we would be ferried up to RAF Longley Lane. One by one the lads turned in and, after visiting the ablutions, I did likewise.

I fell asleep before 'lights out' and got in a good night's sleep, after a traumatic day. I certainly would have no difficulty in remembering my arrival at both Longley Lane and Warton.

The next day we were awoken early by the duty corporal and after washing and shaving, I had my first meal in the Warton cookhouse. All things being considered the food wasn't too bad. For breakfast there was a good selection of cereals, with hot milk in large urns, on a 'help yourself' basis, or you could have porridge. Then there was eggs, bacon, sausage, beans or tomatoes and as many slices of bread and margarine as you could eat. Large unmarked urns contained either tea or coffee. The trouble was, if you went back for a second pot, and you still had some drink left in your pot, you could finish up with a mixture of tea and coffee. After breakfast and rinsing my pot and irons in the obligatory tank of hot water, outside the cookhouse, I made my way back to the hut.

Airmen were drifting outside and started standing in loose formation on the camp road, chattering away amongst themselves. I stood on the edge of the throng. An elderly sergeant ambled up to where everyone was standing and said, in a mild mannered way, 'OK lads, form up in threes', there was an immediate semblance of order, albeit nothing like the smart ranks at West Kirby. Everybody automatically faced down the camp road. The sergeant said, 'By the left, quick march', everyone took off in an ambling sort of a way. I noticed that there was no crunching of boots on the gravel of the road and it was then that I realised everyone, except Chris and me, had rubber soled shoes or boots on their feet.

On later mentioning this fact to one of the airmen, I was told that everyone on the unit had to have their footwear soled and heeled in rubber because of working in the Operations room at Longley Lane and the Central Filter Plotting unit (CFP) at Whittingham Lane. After 'marching' to the MT yard, I followed the others in boarding a more modern RAF coach than the one, which had brought us to Warton the previous night. There were a number of vehicles in the yard.

Three modern type Bedford coaches, the old utility Bedford OB model, two high wheel-based Bedford lorries, which looked fairly new, two wartime Bedford 'Garries', complete with the 'gun turrets' in the cab roof and a very old Austin 'crew coach', with a humped back and a rear entrance. In the open fronted sheds, around the MT yard were various other vehicles, including, smart looking Standard Vanguard cars and a couple of Austin Champ four-wheel drive, off the road vehicles. All the lorries were also four wheel drive. Most of the airmen were milling around the entrances to the coaches, whilst a few climbed into the backs of the lorries, pulling themselves up into the back using the thick 'bull-rope', which hung down from the frame of the vehicle. Those airmen failing to get on a coach were obliged to follow their compatriots onto the lorries. The lorry cabs all seemed to be occupied by NCOs of various ranks. Eventually, one by one, the vehicles started up and moved off, out of the MT yard, turning left towards the main gate of 'No 8 site'. A RAF policeman stood at the stanchion pole, outside the guardroom, raising the bar to allow the convoy of vehicles to pass.

The journey to Longley Lane was quite interesting, seeing the countryside in daylight, which I had traversed the previous evening in the dark. There was plenty to look at. Over the next couple of years the journey would get tedious and boring, as we made the daily trips to and from Longley Lane. The first proper day at the Western Sector Operations Centre was most exciting.

Most of those on my coach were chattering away, whilst at the back of the coach a cards school was in progress, this was, I was to discover a daily event on one or the other of the transport vehicles. I was to find that, a small group of airmen, two of them from Liverpool, did nothing but gamble continuously, even paying other airmen to do their shifts on the plotting table. On several occasions I benefited from their mania for playing poker, taking payment to do their work. How they got away with it I shall never know.

Once out on the highway the more modern vehicles left the others behind and the convoy was strung out as vehicles got through junctions where others had to stop. Eventually we arrived at Longley Lane, where most of us alighted, some stayed on our coach which then left for the CFP. I was not aware on that first day of the separate existence of the CFP at Whittingham Lane.

I followed the group of airmen into the block, descending down the steps and through the entrance. At the police desk I found Chris standing there, the RAF policeman said, 'Are you another new one?', 'Yes corporal', I answered. 'Wait over there with him', he said, pointing to Chris. We stood there watching the airmen file in. As they passed the police desk, each airman handed in a security pass, before either going along one of the corridors on the upper floor, or turning right down the stairs to the lower floor of the block. The airmen passing were of various ranks and included Leading Aircraftsmen, Senior Aircraftsmen, Junior Technicians (with one inverted stripe on each arm) Corporals and Corporal Technicians, Sergeants and a single Flight Sergeant. We also saw several officers come into the block, again of various ranks.

Eventually, the RAF policeman came from behind his counter and closed the large door, 'Right you two', he said, beckoning us towards the police desk, 'Lets have your 1250s'. We took our identity cards out of our tunic pockets and handed them over. The policeman took a couple of blank cards out of a drawer and started filling them in, eventually stamping the card with a stamp which read, 'Royal Air Force Longley Lane'. Addressing us again, he said, 'This is your security pass, don't lose it. Each morning you will hand this in here or else you won't be allowed in the block, do you understand?'. 'Yes Corporal', we answered. 'Sign the card here', he said, pointing to the space allocated on the pass for a signature. We complied with his direction. 'When you leave the building, at any time, you must collect your security pass from the policeman on duty, understood?'. Again we answered in the affirmative. 'Right, go down those stairs and along the corridor facing the bottom of the stairs, the second door on the left is the Admin Office, report there for instructions'. I followed Chris down the stairs.

I suppose that this is as good as any place to describe the underground bunker in which I found myself and where I would be working on a daily basis over the next 21 months of my RAF service.

The 'block', as we called it, was about as big as a medium sized cinema. The whole of the unit was built around a central Operations room. Three-quarters of the building was below ground and the part which protruded above the ground was covered in grass, sloping banks leading up to a flat surface, also covered in grass. Here and there pipes protruded above the ground, but not more than eight or nine inches, these had caps on the top like miniature Chinamen's hats. On one side of the block was the Vehicle Park from which a paved path led down to the bunker entrance. Beyond the bunker entrance the path continued to three wire surrounded compounds.

Each compound was covered in gravel and a dog kennel held centre stage. This was where the police guard-dogs were kept when they were not on duty. At the far side of the dog compounds was an incinerator, surrounded by remnants of burnt items, most of which was burnt paper. Down the side and back of the block the ground fell away, making the sloping sides steeper on those sides. The whole area was surrounded by a wire netting fence, which sloped in at the top and was strung out with barbed wire. I suppose from the air the block would be hard to see, from the nearest point that members of the public could see, the block was simply a large grass covered mound.

Inside the block the light was artificial, there being no windows. Immediately on passing the police desk and going straight forward, a corridor led into the right hand side of the building, the first door on the left was the Meteorological office, a place I was to get to know well. Carrying on down the corridor, another corridor went off to the left, (I'll come back to that corridor later). A door blocked the way and, on opening this door the corridor widened out at an angle on the left, the front being covered with glass windows which sloped out at about 45%. Just in front of the windows were bench tables along the walls, in front of which were stools. From this vantagepoint there was a good view down into the Operations room, which will be described later. The corridor resumed its previous width as it went down the right hand side of the Operations room with glass windows the full length of the left-hand side of the corridor. At the end of the corridor three steps led down to another door through which there was a very short corridor leading to a staircase. Just before reaching that staircase, an opening on the left led down to a mezzanine floor into an area that was known as the 'Tote'.

In the 'Tote' room, the left-hand wall was louvered from top to bottom. Airmen working in this area received information about the projected flights of RAF aircraft, their call-signs, take off times, destinations and estimated arrival times. Their job was to make up words from hundreds of letters on metal shaped thus "∧", the pieces of metal were then slotted through the louvered wall making the displayed information visible to the inside of the Operations room. Erks in this job had to be adept at spelling words back to front, for example 'White Shadow 1' would be set up from the 'Tote' room as '1 wodahS etihW'.

Crossing the mezzanine floor led to another small staircase. At the top, to the right was a staircase leading to the lower floor and matching the staircase at the right-hand side of the building. Turning left along a short corridor led to another door through which were three steps and then another corridor running parallel with the one at the far side of the Operations room, which I have just described. At the far end of this was another widened area, matching the one at the other side of the building. Going through the door at the end of the corridor, there was a corridor leading off to the left. Turning left into the corridor, there were doors on either side. The first door on the left was the entrance to the Control Cabin, known as 'Ops B'. Immediately inside the door were three steps, to the left of which was a large wall map, on which was identified every operational RAF airfield in the UK. Small hooks protruded from the named sites and plaques showing the weather state at each airfield. This room was where the officers controlling operations for Fighter Command Western Sector carried out their duties. The officers sat along bench tables overlooking the Operations room and looking down on the very large maps which were located in that room and on which airmen plotted the flights of all RAF aircraft in the UK. The bench tables were littered with telephones of various colours and toggle switches set into the tabletop.

The officers had the use of opera glasses for closer viewing. At the far side of the Operations room, over the map tables was the louvered wall previously described, displaying aircraft identification information. Leaving the 'Ops B' cabin and turning into the next door left, there was a room set aside for VIPs to sit and view the action in the Operations room. The Sector Commander, a Group Captain and former 'Battle of Britain' ace, would sit there on his visits to the unit. Coming out of that room and turning back right along the corridor, there were two rooms on the left.

The one almost opposite the one just described, was a room which contained various items of training aids, a film projector, fold-up screen, film winding equipment and splicing equipment and an 'Epidiascope' (a device under which solid objects could be placed and their image projected onto a screen). Two airmen usually occupied that room, continuously updating the 'Queens Regulations' manual, I suspect it was a 'skivers' paradise. The next room on the left was the Commanding Officer's office, a room I only visited twice during my stay at RAF Longley Lane.

Carrying on down the corridor and turning left, a door on the left led into the Tele-printer room. Passing that the corridor turned left. In the very corner on the right, a door led into the Officers' Rest Room, I only visited that room once, whilst on fire piquet and out of curiosity. Continuing on the corridor, back in the direction of the police desk, the next door on the right was the Officers toilets, opposite which was the MT (Motor Transport) office. The NCO in charge of the vehicle pool, Corporal Skipper, a full-blown scouse and the double of the film star Norman Rossington manned this office. Lastly, on the right, was the entrance to the police desk. A full circuit of the upper floor has been described.

Opposite the police desk was the staircase to the lower floor, it went down about 10 steps and then a left turn on a small landing and then another 10 steps to the lower level. At the bottom of the steps could be seen a long corridor, half way down which was a set of three steps leading on to the end. Going down that corridor, which was blank on the whole of the right hand side, there were three doors on the left. The first one on the left was a NCO's rest room, next to which was the Administration office, (my best mate, who I was yet to meet, worked in that office). Carrying on, down the three steps and nearly at the bottom, there was a door on the left leading in to the Operations room, (more of that later). A door at the very end of the corridor led into the Radio Direction Finding Plotting room, known to one and all as 'the fixers'. In the room were two identical round tables each showing a section of a map of Great Britain.

The map was of the area covered by the Western Sector, Fighter Command 12 Group. The farthest south on the map was the Bristol Channel, whilst the top of the map finished in the northern part of the Mull of Kintyre. To the east the map showed the central part of England running down the Pennines, whilst on the far west of the map was the Atlantic coast of the Irish Republic and Northern Ireland. At various points on the map, a compass rose was marked out, at the centre of the compass rose was a brass ring. To the side of each compass rose was the name of the Royal Air Force radio direction finding station (RDF), for example, 'Valley', represented the RDF station near to RAF Valley on the isle of Anglesey. There was one for Ronaldsway on the Isle of Man, one at RAF Aldergrove in Northern Ireland and to the north at Stornaway, as well as others to the east. All round the map tables were jack plugs where headsets could be plugged in. An airman, who was in direct contact with the RDF station operator, would man each position.

The plugs were at the opposite side of the table from the compass rose, identifying the RDF station. At the back of the room was a podium, which was raised up, and was normally, manned by a corporal. When an aircraft flying through the Western Sector area made a radio transmission, the aerial at the RDF station would pick up the radio signal.

The airman at these stations sat at a steering wheel on which was a large compass rose. On receiving the radio transmission, the RDF operator would spin his steering wheel, which rotated the RDF aerial. When the transmission was at its highest volume, the operator would read off the compass bearing to the airman at the 'fixer' table at Longley Lane.

Each of the airmen around the table would receive a different compass rose reading. They would reach forward and take hold of the brass ring and pull the ring towards them. Attached to the ring was some heavy-duty twine, weighted under the table, this would be pulled out and stretched across the map. Where all the strings crossed would be the location of the aircraft making the radio transmission. The corporal on the podium, (known as the teller) would read out the map reference through a telephone to an airman in the Operations room who would display the position of the aircraft on a transparent 'fighter' screen. The type of 'fix' would be dependent on the clarity of each transmission. A good clear transmission would result in all the strings on the map crossing at the same point, this was classed as an 'Able' type fix. The weaker the signal from the aircraft, the worse the fix that was shown on the 'fixer' map.

Sometimes the strings were wide apart with several triangular gaps where they all crossed, such a fix needed an experienced eye to work out the aircraft position and there could be an error of many miles on occasions. I spent many hours in the fixer room, at quiet times talking to the operator at the remote RDF station many miles away. We never got on name terms with our colleagues at the RDF stations, they simply called us 'Preston', which was our 'fixer' code name and we called them, 'Valley' or 'Ronaldsway' or whatever station we were plugged in to at the time.

Continuing the tour of the building. To the rear of the fixer room was, what could be termed as, the engine room of the block. A large room contained, air filtering equipment, electricity generators, heating equipment and other machinery that was designed to keep the underground bunker self sufficient in the case of a nuclear attack. In the event of such an attack, all the occupants of the building would be shut in for an unspecified period. Obviously after a while there would be a drain on essentials and it is frightening to think of the consequences of a long stay in the underground bunker.

In the machinery room, one of our colleagues set up a hairdressing business, with the complete approval of the Commanding Officer. Haircuts there were half the price charged at the camp hairdressers, and perhaps a quarter of the cost of a civilian barber, Jack, the airman concerned had served his apprenticeship in 'civvie' street and must have made a small fortune during his National Service. His other claim to fame was that his sister-in-law was a well known pop star of the fifties, every time he went on leave there would be requests from airmen for signed photographs from his sister-in-law. An offshoot from the machinery room was the workshop of the civilian carpenter/handyman, who did the everyday repairs to the structure of the building, clearing blocked drains, changing fluorescent light tubes, etc. On the way out of the machinery room the corridor opposite the one traversed earlier was straight on from the fixer room. Going up this corridor, the right-hand wall was blank for the full length of the corridor, whilst on the left there was a number of doors.

The first door led into the Operations room and was the door, which we all normally used, the corridor on this side of the building being the busiest corridor in the building. I'll return to the Operations room later. There were three steps to go up to the next room on the left, which was the workshop for the civilian workers, employed by the GPO Post Office Telephones. These civilians maintained all of the hundreds of telephone lines, which came through the block. The workshop was 'out of bounds' to all airmen, so it was the one room I never entered, when the block was 'stood down' and we were on fire piquet, the room was always locked.

The next room up the corridor was the office of a RAF Signals Officer, who I will call Flight Lieutenant Godfrey. This officer was a very dour character but treated you like a human being. He did not talk down to you but spoke on your level. When I first arrived at Longley Lane he was a Flying Officer and was promoted during my service there. I found out that he had come up through the ranks and had received his commission after having been a Warrant Officer for many years.

The next room on the left was the favourite of all the lower ranks at Longley Lane, it was the Airmen's Mess room. It was a fairly large room and was equipped with both folding wooden chairs and a number of leather armchairs with wooden arms at the sides. There were a number of small tables and in the top right-hand corner, a fairly large bookcase, this was the station library. I'll come back to the library later. Going out of the mess room and turning left led to the end of the corridor, which took a sharp left turn. In the corner of the corridor was a hatch in the wall and to the left of the hatch, a door led into the kitchen. During the week, three airmen (commonly known in the RAF as 'skivers') manned the kitchen. They served pots of tea or coffee and a selection of buns, cream slices, doughnuts, chocolate eclairs, small packets of biscuits and some rather delicious fruit pies (in individual boxes, which you don't seem to be able to buy these days).

The provisions were delivered from Warton in a NAAFI van each day and presumably were paid for out of mess funds and the money taken from airmen purchasing the goods. No doubt our colleagues were ripping us off, but they provided a service throughout the day. Although they were trained in the same trade as me, they were never seen in the Operations room. I suppose they had a lot of pot washing to do, but, apart from that, they had a fairly cushy time. Whenever I had to do either fire piquet duties or late night flying duties, (known to one and all as 'night binds'), I got to see the inside of the kitchen. Someone always got the job of doing sandwiches or a fry-up for the rest of the lads, after the block had stood down at night. I generally drew the short straw for some unknown reason.

Leaving the kitchen and continuing along the corridor, the next room was the WAAF's toilets. Although we had no permanent attachment of WAAFs to our unit, on many weekends we had visits from various Royal Auxiliary Air Force squadrons, which included a number of females. Such visits led to some excitement amongst my colleagues, and I must admit I was smitten on a couple of occasions by good-looking young ladies in the uniform of the auxiliary air force. One particular female corporal from the city of Bath really made me go weak at the knees, the interest was not mutual, she was a very serious young lady, who was only interested in the job in hand. A funny incident, which I will relate later, occurred in the WAAF's toilets.

On the opposite side of the corridor was a fairly large room, which was used for training purposes. There was a movie projector and screen in the room and I got to know the room and its equipment very well, later in my career at Longley Lane.

At the end of the corridor was the staircase, which led back up to the upper floor and where the journey around the block started. On the mezzanine landing was the entrance to the male toilets, with its four traps, urinal and sinks, a good place for skiving and having a quiet read, except at shift changes, when the place was well used.

Finally, back to the Operations room. By far the biggest area in the block, it was the reason for the whole of the block's existence. As you entered the 'Ops' room, from the left-hand corridor, immediately on the left were racks of telephone headsets, which airmen collected on the way in to take up their plotting duties. A large map of Great Britain dominated the room. The map must have been about fifteen feet across, from East to West and about twenty feet from North to South. All around the map table were units on which stood the plaques used to display the aircraft information, row upon row of small pieces of metal, with numbers and letters painted on them. There were racks, similar to those that hold snooker cues, holding the various sizes of plotting rods. An airman going on duty in the

'Ops' room, having collected his headset, would next take hold of a plotting rod and plug into the jack-plug at the side of the airman he was relieving. There would be a few minutes whilst the new plotter assimilated the current situation. When he was ready to take over, he would give a signal to the person being relieved, who would then unplug and leave the 'Ops' room, usually accompanied by his 'raid orderly', i.e., the airman who prepared the plaques to the instructions of the person plotting. A new 'raid orderly' would then take up the duties, assisting the new plotter.

At the back of the map table, hung on the wall, which formed the bottom part of the outside of the 'tote' (previously described), was a large colour change clock.

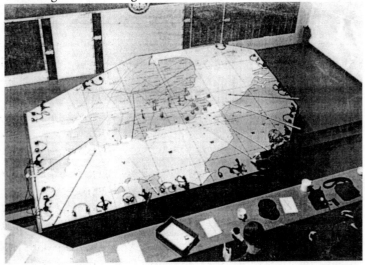

An operations room similar to that at RAF Longley Lane. The Colour Change clock can just be seen at the top centre of the picture.

The clock was synchronised with a set of three lights, on display in a frame at the head of the map table. As the minute hand of the clock traversed around the clock face, it went through five-minute segments, painted, red, blue or yellow. When the clock hand left the red segment and went into the blue, the synchronised lights changed from red to blue.

The wall over the top of the map, facing the 'Ops' cabin, on the upper floor, was louvered from top to bottom and the displays put there by members of the 'tote' team could be read by the officers in 'Ops B'. On the left hand side of the 'Ops' room was what was known as a, 'Fighter Screen'. This was a massive sheet of plastic, with a map of the Western Sector, (as described on the 'fixer' map table). The screen was grid referenced and lit from the top, the light penetrated the plastic and highlighted the engraved detail of the map and grid references. Airmen using the screen had to be very versatile, as, using 'China-graph' pencils, they had to write in reverse on the screen, a difficult task. I tried it on many occasions and my reverse writing was terrible. Drawn arrows represented the latest position of an aircraft as tracked by the people in the 'fixer' room, from information supplied by the RDF stations.

At the front of the 'Ops' room, below the 'Ops B' cabin, was a series of smaller cabins, looking for all the world like a modern day conservatory. The only use I saw these cabins put to was for storage. In one of them small group of 'skivers' spent their day, repainting the small metal inserts for the plotting plaques.

To the left of the room, there was a small cabin, which was occupied by the duty corporal or sergeant, in charge of the 'Ops' room. In the cabin was a PBX (telephone) switchboard and a wire recorder, (as described at the very beginning of my story).

When fully manned, the 'Ops' room was a hive of activity, with plotting rods dipping up and down as airmen plotted RAF aircraft flying all over the UK. As you could imagine, it was not a quiet place, with plotters shouting their instructions to the 'raid orderlies' and the clatter of the metal plaques and plotting arrows on the surface of the huge map. Can you imagine what it was like to come from training and find yourself plotting real aircraft? The duty NCO's usually started new plotters on the quieter regions of the country, you had to be no less than a Senior Aircraftman to plot on the south-eastern section of the map.

The description of the block may have been tedious to the reader, but it is necessary to my story, as many of the later incidents to which I refer occurred in the various parts of the underground building.

Later in my service I was to visit the Caledonian Sector Operations Centre, at Barnton Quarry, near Edinburgh, and in 1999 I visited the Southern Area SOC, at Kelvedon Hatch. These two blocks were almost identical underground, but totally different to Longley Lane. Nearby the SOC was the Whittingham Lane CFP (Central Filter Plotting) and down near the A6, but well hidden in the countryside, was the underground signals unit, known as QQ. More of Barnton Quarry and QQ later.

6. RAF Longley Lane (2)

(Where I become a proper 'erk')

The block had no facilities for mass feeding, the small kitchen was only capable of providing snacks and hot drinks. We must have been unique in the services, in that every day we dined in a restaurant in the centre of Preston. There were two lunch sittings, known, as you might have guessed, as 'first lunch' and 'second lunch'. You were allocated to a lunch break each day and so usually relieved, from whatever you were doing, about ten minutes before the departure of the coaches into Preston. As only half of the unit went on each lunch break, we were fortunate to have the use of the coaches every day. After collecting our security passes at the police desk, we boarded the coaches and were ferried down into the centre of Preston.

The 'Mayfair' restaurant was on Fishergate and the main part of the restaurant, which was open to the general public, was on the ground floor. Officers and senior NCOs dined in the main restaurant. The rest of us, 'the scrubbers' or 'minions' dined on the first and second floor. We sat at tables with real tablecloths and proper place settings, and we had waitress service. Meals were ferried up to the upper floors by a 'dumb waiter' lift and each day, the waitresses served over two hundred hungry airmen a three-course meal. The food was, on the whole, very good, the trouble was that, we could have, for example, fish, chips and peas at the 'Mayfair' and then when we got back to RAF Warton in the evening, find that the exact same meal was being served in the cookhouse.

There was usually an alternative meal choice each day, from the main menu. Every day, before serving the meal, waitresses would bring round the menu for the following day. The menu would show the main meal and the alternative. If you wanted the alternative, you told the waitress and she would issue you with a small ticket, somewhat like the old cinema tickets. Printed on the ticket was the wording '*Mayfair Guild*' and a serial number. Theoretically the system should have worked, if you didn't hand in a ticket you got the main meal, if you handed the waitress a ticket, you were served the alternative.

Twenty tickets issued the previous day should have meant twenty alternative meals. The person who thought up the system had forgotten one factor, they were dealing with a load of young wags, set on knackering the system! Every day, they would finish up with a shortage of main meals and too many alternative meals, as airmen who had taken a ticket the previous day for the alternative meal, failed to hand in their ticket, claiming to have ordered the main meal. The manager of the restaurant, one, Luigi (of unknown extraction) could not understand why his system was not working and daily went in to apoplectic rages, as his catering was thrown into disarray by mischievous airmen.

As was the practice in normal cookhouses, throughout the RAF, on one day each week, a duty officer would come round the upper floors of the restaurants, speaking to each airman and asking the well known question, 'any complaints?'. Luiggi would accompany the duty officer and again, certain airmen would take the opportunity of driving Luiggi into an early grave by making some complaint. Whenever someone complained, Luiggi would throw his arms up in the air and protest in the manner of an Italian footballer, all this to the great amusement of most of the airmen present. Luiggi bit on every occasion and never seemed to realise that he was being set up.

Most of the waitresses were middle aged to elderly, they all wore black uniforms with small white aprons, in the fashion of the Lyons' 'nippies'. One however was an attractive Scots lady, who must have been in her early thirties, and on whom I had a bit of a crush, I'm afraid. She got plenty of attention from the lads and was always having the strings of her apron pulled as she passed by the lecherous airmen she waited upon.

On the opposite side of the road from the restaurant, over the top of some shops was an office. The windows of the office displayed the word '*KALAMAZOO*', in curved gold lettering. Some quite attractive young ladies worked in the offices and the window seats in the restaurant were fought over by the dining 'erks'. We spent long periods of time waving at the girls, and receiving their waves back. Every time I hear the Glenn Miller tune, '*I've got a gal in Kalamazoo*', I think of the young ladies in the office opposite our dining venue in Preston, incredibly they will all now be in their sixties.

On the odd occasion, I got to dine on the lower floor, the main part of the restaurant. When dining with the NCO's and officers, one had to be on the best behaviour. The time when there was an overflow situation was usually when we had auxiliary air force people on attachment to our unit.

After lunch each day, if the weather was fine, there would be groups of airmen wandering the town centre of Preston, mainly window-shopping, but often engaged in other activities. Outside the main post office in Fishergate, there was a large oval post box. Fitted to the side of the post box was a stamp-issuing machine, which gave out, (believe it or not), halfpenny stamps. Someone found out that, if you put one halfpenny into the machine, and then yanked on the stamp as it emerged from the machine, about six or seven stamps could be obtained. The machine was well patronised by airmen. My aunt once asked me why I always put halfpenny stamps on my letters, and, many of the letters I sent to my girlfriend Elsie, (later to become my wife), bear halfpenny stamps on the envelopes, we still have the evidence. The machine was never rectified, in the twenty-one months I was at RAF Longley Lane. Whether the GPO knew about it and felt sorry for the underpaid airmen that patronised the machine, I will never know.

Down one of the side streets in Preston, there was what was known at the time as a 'Turf-Accountant'. Betting was illegal in those days and everything had to be done surreptitiously. I personally never placed any bets, but a number of my colleagues were convinced they had ways of getting rich through betting on the horses. Every day they would leave the Mayfair restaurant and make straight for the 'bookies'. They would look around furtively, before entering the side door of the building and going upstairs to the office of the 'Turf-Accountant'.

One lad, John Devonshire, was always expounding his theories of how to win large amounts of money, he had systems worked out for betting on the football pools and the racehorses. John was a scruffy looking individual, his complexion could only be described as greasy, his face was covered in acne and blackheads, yet he spoke so upper-class it was unbelievable. One day I was obliged to act as escort when John was put on a charge for reading a newspaper on parade. Each morning, we had to assemble outside our huts at Warton and march down to the MT yard. We were an untidy shuffling mob, far removed from the smart turn out at West Kirby. For a start, because of our working in the 'Ops' room, our shoes and boots were rubber soled. There was no crunching on the gravel, we were the 'silent' mob.

Anyhow I digress... One morning, we were being marched down to the MT yard by an elderly sergeant, 'Granny' Smith. As we traversed the camp roads we passed an officer going in the opposite direction, the sergeant shouted 'Eyes right' and threw up a salute to the young officer. We had got about ten yards past the officer when a cry came from the rear of 'Halt'.

Suddenly the officer came into our midst and dragged Devonshire out by the lapel of his jacket.

'Sergeant! I want this man charging.'

'Yes Sir' said Sergeant Smith, 'What with?'

'Reading a newspaper on parade,' replied the officer.

Royal Air Force		R.A.F. Form 252
CHARGE REPORT		

CHARGE

Charge against No...

(Unit)..

PLACE AND DATE OF OFFENCE :

OFFENCE	WITNESSES

Signature of person preferring the charge...........................

(Unit).. (Date)..........................

(Disposal of charge to be recorded overleaf.)

The infamous RAF Form 252

A couple of days later, I found myself detailed by another sergeant, to act as one of the escorts to John Devonshire, when he appeared in front of the Commanding Officer of RAF Longley Lane.

We stood lined up in the corridor outside the CO's office. Suddenly the door of the office opened and Sergeant Freeman came out, he was the youngest sergeant on the unit, a very smart individual, who wore frameless glasses. The sergeant said loudly, 'Prisoner and escort, attention!' Devonshire, the other escort and me stiffened to attention. The sergeant gave the turn to the left command and then marched us at the double, into the CO's office. Following the sergeant's commands, we found ourselves in front of the CO's desk.

Devonshire was given the command to remove his headgear. Sergeant Freeman then said, 'Sir! Leading Aircraftman Devonshire'. We stood stiffly at attention during the whole of the hearing. The Commanding Officer, Squadron Leader Butcher, read out the charge to John Devonshire and on finishing said, 'What have you to say in your defence Devonshire?'

In his upper class voice, John said that he had been marching down the road on the way to the MT yard. He continued, 'I had the Daily Telegraph under my left arm Sir, suddenly I looked down and saw the name of someone, I knew quite well, in the newspaper. I don't know what possessed me, but I took the newspaper from under my arm to get a better look at the article in which the name appeared. That's when the officer dragged me out by the scruff of my neck'.

Squadron Leader Butcher looked at Devonshire for a few moments and then said, 'Is that all you have to say Airman?'

'Yes Sir', replied Devonshire.

The C.O. then gave Devonshire a sentence of five days jankers. We were then marched out of his office. I felt that I had been on a charge, I was so nervous. That was the only time I was involved in any sort of disciplinary proceedings whilst at Longley Lane.

'Granny' Smith, the sergeant in charge, on the day of Devonshire's misdemeanour, was the oldest sergeant on the unit, in fact he retired the service during my time at Longley Lane. He was a mild mannered person who never gave us much bother. He must have only been in his late forties or early fifties, but he looked really old to us young ones.

One day when we were standing down, at the end of our day's duty, we were all instructed to assemble on parade in the car park. When we were all lined up in threes, the C.O. came out and addressed us. It would seem that some wag had sent off for a hearing aid, which had arrived at Sergeant Smith's married quarters, delivered by a very persistent salesman. The C.O. said that, unless the culprit owned up, the whole unit would be confined to camp, on the next 36-hour break. This meant that I and many of the others would not be able to get home on pass. No one owned up at the material time and we were not confined to camp, as threatened, so, whether someone had owned up, or the C.O.'s threat was only a token gesture to Sergeant Smith, I do not know. It was just one of the many funny incidents I recall from my time at Longley Lane.

I well remember my first Christmas in the RAF. On the day before we broke up for Christmas grant, we had all been to the Mayfair Restaurant for lunch. Luigi had done us proud. We had a magnificent Christmas dinner, complete with Christmas crackers and fancy hats and the meal was a full 'Monty', with all the usual favourites being served. When we got back to the unit, I was sent on 'fixers'. I took up my position on the map table and sat there with my headphones. There was nothing flying and most of the operators were talking idle chatter to their colleagues at the RDF stations around the country. I was on the RAF Valley line and had heard nothing from the airman at the other end of the line since I had taken up my duty.

Suddenly a voice came on the line and said, 'Are you there Preston?'

I answered in the affirmative.

'Have you had your Christmas dinner yet?' enquired the voice.

'Yes', I replied.

'What have you had?' said the friendly voice, who I assumed was the RDF airman at RAF Valley. I then started to reel off what I had had for my Christmas lunch. Halfway through describing the menu, I suddenly became aware that my chattering colleagues had gone suspiciously quiet. I looked around the room and then saw an airman crouched down beside the reserve table. He was plugged in to the identical position that I was on, on the main table. I suddenly realised that I had been describing my Christmas lunch to someone who was less than twelve feet away. Once the other airmen realised that I had tumbled to the situation, a laugh went up. I had been the victim of a regular prank pulled by the more experienced airmen at Longley Lane.

On the main plotting tables, it was not possible to speak to the airman who was relaying the information to you, the line was one way, so only the ear-pieces were live on the head-sets. If you missed a plot, then there was no asking for a repeat, you just had to wait for the next plot on that particular aircraft and rectify the matter. New airmen often started out as 'raid' orderlies, i.e., preparing the plaques on the shouted instructions of the plotters.

At certain times life could be hectic, particularly in the summer, when lots of aircraft were flying. It was at times like that when a break was welcome. I once saw an auxiliary air force WAAF, pull her headset off and throw it on the table, scattering some of the plaques and directional arrows. A corporal whisked her off and we never saw her again. What happened to her I don't know, if she had been a regular, she would have been in serious trouble, as it was she was probably dismissed from the service.

On some summer nights, we would be kept back late, plotting into the late evening and sometimes the early morning. These were referred to as 'night binds'. There was no extra pay, you were simply given the next morning off from duties.

In winter and whenever there was severe weather, causing flying to be restricted, life could get boring. I have seen times when we have sat at the plotting table for a full shift with nothing on the table. In these situations time dragged and it was great to see your relief arrive. We spent one hour on the table, or at other duties, such as in the fixer room, and one hour off. The one-hour off was often interrupted by the arrival of the administration sergeant, who delighted in finding idle hands something to do. We lowly 'erks' did the entire interior cleaning of the block and the floors and corridors in particular, were a credit to our prowess. We had been well trained at square-bashing, in the art of wielding the dreaded 'bumper'. Many is the happy hour I have spent with a colleague, armed with a large can of Mansion polish, a stick, for the flicking of the said polish and our trusty bumper. The corridor floors in particular gleamed. After Sgt. Smith retired a new sergeant took his place. The old adage 'different as chalk and cheese' jumps to mind. Where Sgt Smith had been quiet and well mannered, his replacement was loud and uncouth. He was nearly as round as he was tall and always wore a best blue jacket, the bottom of which splayed out like a ballerina's tou-tou. He delighted in coming into the airmen's mess room and spoiling our rest breaks. His orders were short and terse. He would point at a couple of airmen and say, 'you and you, corridors'. That meant that those selected would spend the next hour polishing one of the corridors. On one occasion, he said to a couple of the lads, 'you two, shit-houses', to which one of the airmen said in a protesting manner, 'sergeant, I did the shit-houses yesterday', waving his thumb over his shoulder in the direction of the door, the sergeant simply said, 'shit-houses'. There was no arguing with him.

This sergeant had come to us direct from a Far East posting. He had spent some considerable time in Singapore and did not seem to like his current posting. He was not vindictive and I never knew him to charge anyone, he expected to be obeyed however and anyone choosing to argue, simply was shouted down. The lads at the block did not dislike him, in fact one day, a number of us saved him from getting into serious trouble. On that day, he went into Preston on the 'first lunches' transport, but failed arrive for the journey back to Longley Lane. When he turned up for the return transport from the second lunch, he was well and truly sozzled. Some airmen managed to get him onto the transport without him being seen by a superior officer and when the vehicle, which was a high-wheeled Bedford 3 tonner, arrived at the block, he was left in the back covered with some tarpaulin. By the time the end of the day's duty came about, he had slept off the drink and was back to his usual uncouth self. For all of his brusqueness and bawling, he was not a bad person at heart, I've often wondered what became of him.

Richard Matthews was a MT driver. He was about 6ft 5ins tall and the spitting image of the film star Burt Lancaster. Basically, 'Big Rick', as he was known, was a bully. One of his favourite tricks was to grab someone by the flesh of the inner thigh, squeeze really hard, until the victim yelled out in pain. This was usually accompanied by him saying to the unfortunate he had chosen, 'All right, pal?'. If you were the chosen one, you obviously were not all right. Like most bullies he always picked on someone smaller than he was and anyone below the rank of corporal was fair game. He himself was a lowly AC1 and remained so for the whole of the time I knew him.

One day, I was on my rest period and sitting in one of the few leather armchairs in the mess-room. Every day, we had a selection of the morning papers and I had just finished reading one when Big Rick entered the room. He was carrying a mug of tea in one hand and a plate in the other. On the plate were a vanilla slice and a chocolate Penguin biscuit. I stood out of my chair to lean over to swap newspapers, as I did so, Big Rick slid into the armchair at the back of me. I don't know what possessed me, but I turned on him and, 'Now then 'chuff', that's my chair'.

Big Rick looked at me and said, 'You what?'

I replied, 'You heard 'chuff', that's my seat'.

Just as though someone had waved a magic wand, a silence came over the room, everyone stopped talking and looked in my direction. Big Rick stood up, turned round to the chair and carefully balanced his pot of tea and the plate on the leather seat and, looking around him stated to the onlookers, 'That's my chair, I'm going to sort Voysey out'.

Again I do not know what possessed me, for I pushed Big Rick in his stomach, catching him off balance. He staggered back and fell into the armchair, sitting on his pot of tea and crushing his vanilla slice and chocolate Penguin. I turned on my heel and dashed out of the mess-room. Turning right, I ran down the corridor and into the Ops room. Grabbing a headset I went and plugged in at the side of one of the plotters. 'I've come to take you off', I said breathlessly.

'I've only just come on replied the plotter'.

'It's OK,' I said, 'You've got an extra break'.

I looked toward the door of the Ops room, Big Rick was leaning through the door, shaking his fist at me and mouthing, 'I'll get you Voyse'.

As a MT driver, he was not allowed in the Ops room, so I knew I was safe for the time being. Overlooking the Ops room were the duty officers, so, even if he had been able to enter, anything he did would be seen by the officers and the duty NCO in the Ops room. I had a temporary reprieve, but over the next few weeks I lived with the feelings that a condemned prisoner must experience. Every time I went round a corner, I had to look round first, to see if Big Rick was in the vicinity.

When boarding the transport, I always waited until a corporal or sergeant was in the vicinity, shadowing them into the vehicle and sitting as close as I could. As the weeks went by, I was surprised that Big Rick did not waylay me, he seemed to forget the incident and life went back to normality. I even plucked up enough courage to ride in his cab one day, on that occasion, I got away with a gripped thigh and an, 'Alright Pal?'. I suppose that one-day, Big Rick met up with someone bigger than he was and came unstuck, I will never know.

Another MT driver, a person of a totally different character to Big Rick, was a lad called Brian. One day on the private road, which led down, through a farmyard to the QQ block, Brian allowed one of the Service Policemen to have a drive of his 'garry'. These vehicles were very high off the ground and it was quite a feat climbing into the cab. They were four wheel drive, which was very fortunate on this occasion as, the SP dropped the lorry off the road, into a ditch on the left-hand side of the road. Everyone in the vehicle's back was thrown about, luckily no one was injured. The lorry's front nearside wheel was well and truly in the ditch. The offside rear wheel was clear of the ground, but luckily, with some help from pushing airmen, and the vehicle's four wheel drive system, Brian managed to get his lorry back on to the dirt track road. If it had been a wet day, it is odds on the vehicle would have remained stuck. Much as we did not like most Service Policemen, none of the airmen present breathed a word about the incident, mainly for Brian's good and not the SP's. Brian was a fool to give in to the SP, who had no driving licence and he was lucky the vehicle was not damaged. I suppose both of them could have been in severe trouble had the incident been found out.

On another occasion, Brian found himself in trouble because of his easygoing nature. Most days, the transports followed the same route to and from Warton and Longley Lane. One day however, some of the lads persuaded Brian to try a different route. After leaving Longley Lane and arriving at the A6, instead of turning left towards Preston, which was the recognised route, Brian went to the right, across the A6 and turned immediately left into a very narrow country lane. It was a lovely evening and everyone appeared to be enjoying the change of scenery as we bounced along this unclassified road. Suddenly there was a loud crashing noise and the whole of the framework, which supported the canvas on the back of the lorry, was bent backwards. Brian had driven his lorry through a railway arch, which was very low and dipped sharply on each side of the road. Brian's lorry had taken on a swept back look, which was not exactly the type of streamlining which would be appreciated by the RAF. Poor old Brian finished up on a charge for that fiasco and did a number of nights on 'jankers'. He kept to the recognised routes after that day.

On another occasion, we were travelling along the Lytham by-pass road, towards Freckleton. Brian was really getting his foot down. Suddenly, we 'erks' in the back saw a Wolesley police car closing up on our lorry. One of the lads ran to the front of the vehicle and banged on the metal rear of the cab. Brian slid the glass shutter back and asked what was wrong. He was made aware of the situation. He immediately slowed down to the speed limit for his vehicle and the police car overtook us. Suddenly an arm came out of the police car window, waving up and down. At the same time a light on the car roof lit up with the words 'POLICE STOP' in red.

Brian obeyed the sign, pulling his lorry into the left-hand side of the road. A large policeman stepped out of the car and walked slowly up towards Brian's cab. Brian jumped down from the vehicle and for the next five minutes got a right ear bending from the copper. We, in the back of the lorry, could not hear what was being said, but presumed that Brian would get a ticket. He was lucky, he didn't. As the conversation finished, the policeman raised his voice and said, 'And don't let it happen again'. We thought that was the end of the affair, but instead of returning to his car, the policeman came round to the rear of the vehicle. Climbing up on to the step at the back of the lorry, he looked at the now quiet bunch of 'erks' and said, 'You lot had better watch it. I could knock you all off for perverting the course of justice. Next time keep your noses out of it'. With that, he climbed down and returned to his car. Apparently in those days, a vehicle had to be followed for at least a mile for a speeding charge to stick, our warning to Brian had stopped the policeman's bit of enjoyment.

Whenever we had to return by lorry, rather than coach, we always seemed to have a singsong. Mostly the songs were of the type usually sung by Rugby players. I got to know all sorts of rude songs and can still remember the words to most of them. One of the songs we sang was based on the limerick type rhyme, 'There was a young man from Calcutta' etc., each verse being sung by a different individual was followed by everyone singing the chorus, 'That was a horrible rhyme, sing us another one, just like the other one, sing us another one do'. Then another airman would kick in with a verse. I have known that type of singing to go on nearly all the way from Longley Lane to Warton, without a verse being repeated.

In winter, travelling back in the back of the lorries was sometimes a nightmare if it was raining, we had to have the canvas down at the back, but water still managed to get in. If it was snow, it was worse, we would all huddle together at the cab end of the vehicle's back, both for warmth and to avoid the wet. In winter it was always cold in the back of the lorries and airmen pushed and shoved to get on to the coaches, which, although not much warmer, at least had some illumination and gave you the opportunity to have a read if you wished.

The issuing out of security passes at the end of each day's work, was done in alphabetical order. Yours truly, having a name beginning with 'V', invariably got his pass amongst the last. Consequently on cold wet nights, it was the same band of 'erks' who finished up in the back of the lorries. Additionally on stand down for 36 hour passes, we at the backend of the alphabet, would miss the Ribble service bus into Preston to start our pass. Inevitably we would go on the transport as far as the Fulwood cross-roads in Preston and alight there to start 'thumbing' it home.

One day, some of us reached the end of our tether and we decided to do something about it. I volunteered to be the spokesman. I went to the police desk, my heart pounding in my chest. The policeman at the desk was the sergeant in charge of the SPs. I faltered but then from somewhere plucked up the courage to speak to the sergeant. 'Sergeant' I said, 'Can I ask you a question?'. The sergeant looked up and raised his eyebrows in an answer which I took to mean, 'Yes'. 'You know when the security passes are given out each day?' I said, 'we at the end of the alphabet are always the last to leave the block. We always finish up on the lorries and on pass nights, we invariably miss the bus into Preston'. The sergeant continued to look at me and simply said 'Well?'. I continued, 'Would it be possible for the passes to be called out in reverse order every so often, to make it fairer?'. The sergeant looked back down at his desk and dismissed me by simply saying, 'F... Off'. I reported back to my colleagues accordingly.

One of the MT drivers was named Joe, he was always in trouble. Whenever you saw Joe after the evening meal, he was invariably on his way down to the guardroom in full kit, on his way to do jankers. Joe's problem was drink, if he went out at night, into Blackpool or Lytham, he generally returned in a drunken state. With the drink went bravado. If he had been the sort who had a quiet drink every night and then was able to walk past the guardroom in an orderly manner, he would have had no trouble. The problem was that Joe would alight from the bus, outside the camp gates, and then weave his way into the site. Usually he was not able to get past the guardroom without being stopped by the police. Once stopped Joe could not contain himself, and always let the RAF policeman who had challenged him know what he thought of him and his colleagues. Joe's night would end with him being locked up in the guardroom overnight. The following morning he would appear before the C.O. and then he was back on jankers. The cycle seemed as though it would carry on. He would serve his period of being confined to camp, then, on the first night out, he would go on a binge and end the night under arrest.

One night, everyone knew that Joe should have been on jankers. He was seen going out of the camp by the hole in the back fence. That was the last any of us saw of Joe. Apparently he got himself drunk in Blackpool and stole a car. He drove the car into RAF Kirkham, another base near to Blackpool, and crashed into the stanchion pole outside their guardroom. He was immediately arrested and faced not only charges made by the service police, but charges of stealing a car, which involved the civilian police. We heard on the grapevine that Joe had been sentenced to imprisonment in the 'glasshouse' at Colchester. When sober Joe was a great guy, a pleasant Geordie who was everybody's friend. He wasn't violent with drink, he just was not frightened of anyone.

Another lad who disappeared from Warton was an Irish lad. He had joined the RAF as a regular, even though he was a citizen of Southern Ireland. Anyhow, one evening word got around that Paddy was giving all his kit away. He had made it known to his mates that he was going home on leave to Ireland and that he was not coming back. He was true to his word, we never saw him again.

One evening, one of the lads named Derek, came into the NAAFI and one of the others said, 'What are you doing here Derek, I thought you was turning in early?'. Apparently Derek had been feeling under the weather and had said he was having an early night. Derek then told us that a new airman had arrived and had been brought to the hut where Derek was, by a RAF policeman. Derek had been in bed reading when the airman entered the hut. When he had been shown his bed-space, the new airman had unpacked all of his kit and stowed it away in the bedside lockers. Derek said he had tried to make conversation, but the new lad only gave the briefest of answers to whatever Derek asked. As soon as his kit was stowed away, the new airman changed into his PT kit, shorts and vest. Thinking he was a bit of a fitness freak, Derek had asked the new airman if he was going to do some exercises. The new lad had said 'Yes'. He then proceeded to climb onto his bed, then crossing his legs into a Yoga position, had just sat staring at the opposite wall in complete silence. Derek had stood it so long, but then felt uncomfortable, so he had got out of bed and got dressed and come down to the NAAFI

We later learned that the new airman was named David and he hailed from Harrogate. He had just spent five years at university and, on completing his course had been called up for National Service. David was a nice lad, but somewhat eccentric. He never ate the cooked food served up in the cookhouse, but generally ate cereals onto which he poured all sorts of health foods, which he brought from home. The first time David showed his face in the NAAFI, he spotted the piano and went and sat at the keyboard. Some of the lads gathered around in anticipation of a singsong, however, when David started to play, it was heavy classical music that came from the piano. David was a real intellectual. He kept to himself, but would carry out a conversation with anyone who spoke to him first. As you can imagine, he was a bit of a loner.

One day however, an airman arrived at Warton, who was on the same plane as David. This airman had been based in the British sector of Berlin in Germany, and we found later that he had been involved in listening in to Russian telephone and radio conversations. He spoke fluent Russian and, as his name was Henry, he was christened 'Russian Henry' by the lads on the unit. Russian Henry and David would play chess and get involved in long discussions of a serious nature, no one else would be inclined to join their conversations. One day, rumours got around that David and Russian Henry were going to hold a séance that evening. The venue for the séance was one of the empty Nissen huts, which lined the road opposite our huts, there was an open invitation for anyone to attend. By that time I had made friends with a young man from Bolton, Ted, who worked in the Administration office at Longley Lane.

He was to become my number one mate from the day we met. We went everywhere together, the camp cinema, or the cinema in St. Anne's-on-Sea, or on the odd trips we made into Blackpool. Anyway, Ted and I decided that we would attend the séance, set up by David and Russian Henry. Along with a number of other interested erks, we made our way to the Nissen hut that was to be used. In the centre of the otherwise empty hut, a table had been positioned, with about eight chairs around the table. It was dark and there were candles placed in various niches around the hut.

In the centre of the table was a wineglass and in a circle around the edge of the table were 'Lexicon' cards in alphabetical order. David was at one end of the table and Russian Henry was at the other end. Volunteers were requested to fill the spare seats around the table and several of the lads sat down. Most of them were grinning and the rest of us, who were spectators, were in a light-hearted mood. Russian Henry asked for silence and we all complied with the request, although there was a bit of sniggering going off. Those sitting at the table were asked to place their fingers on the inverted wineglass, which they did. David then went into a sort of Yoga trance and whilst facing the centre of the table, he had his eyes closed. Everyone was looking at David. Suddenly he said, 'Is anybody there?'. Everyone, with the exception of Russian Henry, had grins on their faces. David repeated himself, saying once more, 'Is anybody there?'. Suddenly all the grins disappeared as the wineglass started to vibrate and move. It travelled across to the table to the letter 'Y' and then across to the letter 'E' and then to the letter 'S'. I had a most uncomfortable feeling and goose pimples started to come up on my arms. I looked at Ted and he had a most serious look on his face and I remember the candles being reflected in the lenses of his glasses. David then asked who was trying to make contact.

Once again the wineglass started to move and slowly but surely, spelled out the name 'BRIDIE'. At that point I had seen enough and, tapping Ted on the shoulder, I motioned for him to follow me out of the Nissen hut. It was all very scary. Ted and I made our way to the NAAFI, leaving the others to find out who 'BRIDIE' was. I never got involved again with anything like that.

Another time when I had a scary experience, was when I was on fire piquet at the QQ site. This was an underground bunker that contained a massive telephone exchange, through which all of the lines for the SOC at Longley Lane, and the CFP at Whittington Lane went. It was a weird place situated way out in the country and accessed through a farmyard and along a very narrow private road. A perimeter fence surrounded the bunker and there were two large gates covered in wire netting. To the side of the bunker was a large garage or workshop type Nissen hut, with two big doors at the end nearest to the perimeter fence gates. Inside the Nissen hut there was just a few chairs, a table and a pot-bellied stove. There was a separate room at the opposite end of the hut to the entrance doors, which was used as a kitchen. A sink unit was situated under a metal-framed window and to the right of the unit was the back door of the hut, which was of normal size.

Fire piquet duties at this site consisted mainly of sitting in the hut and reading books or magazines, when the weather was bad, or if it was dark, or, on summer evenings, sitting in the evening sunshine, enjoying the fresh air, until darkness fell.

Every hour we were supposed to enter the bunker via the concrete entrance, just to the rear of the Nissen hut, and wander around the underground establishment checking that the place was all right. We were supposed to stay awake all night, but most people took blankets and, having pushed a couple of chairs together, had a 'kip'.

The usual fire piquet crew consisted of two 'erks' and a RAF policeman. The policeman usually did nothing at all except give out orders, like, 'make a pot of tea' or, 'go and check the block', etc. Anything like work was done by the 'erks'.

My first experience at QQ, was in fact my very first fire piquet duty. That night I was on duty with a lad named Don from Barnsley and a Welsh 'snowdrop' (RAF Policeman). Taffy was quite friendly, it was the first time I had had to do any duties which brought me into close contact with an SP and being a corporal, I was still a little in awe of my newly found Welsh friend. He had instructed us in our duties and shown us around the underground establishment. The place was very weird, there were racks upon racks of telephone equipment, wiring went in all directions and there was a continual electrical humming accompanied by whirring and clicking noises, as the automatic telephone exchange did its work. The furthest that you could go into the bunker was the emergency lighting room, which was quite a way from the main entrance. The room was a large bare one and massive batteries took up the centre of the floor. If the mains lighting failed, these batteries provided emergency lighting throughout the building and presumably provided enough power to operate the automatic telephone exchange.

On doing our first check, we were instructed by the SP to lock the bunker doors behind us on every occasion that we carried out a check. The first time was not too bad, it was still light outside and Don and I felt quite confident with one another's company. We made our way through the strange building, switching lights on and off, as we entered the various rooms of the block. Once lights were switched off, you were in total blackness, other than in the main exchange room, where little red and green lights were constantly flickering on and off as telephone calls were routed through the system. Even in there, the light emitted was minimal. It was a pretty weird place.

Just before we were due to make our second check, the Welsh policeman, who was sitting in an armchair reading a book, said 'Has anyone said anything to you about Eric the ghost?'

We looked at him anxiously and in unison said 'No'.

Taffy looked back at his book and said, 'Oh well it doesn't matter then'. Don and I looked at one another, we both had worried looks on our faces.

'What about Eric the ghost then?' said Don.

'Its perhaps better that you don't know about it', said Taffy.

We were both well and truly concerned by this time. I looked at the corporal and said, 'Is it supposed to be haunted around, or something?'

The SP continued to read for a short time and then said, 'Well if you really want to know, a GPO telephone engineer was once electrocuted inside the block and some airmen claim to have heard a motorbike start up outside the Nissen hut in the middle of the night, and on checking outside, there has been nothing there. The thing was the man who was killed used to come to work on a motorbike and it is thought that it is him that haunts the site.' Don looked at me in an anxious manner and I felt goose bumps coming up on my arms. A few more minutes passed and then Taffy said, 'Isn't it time for your next check?'

Don and I put on our greatcoats and picking up the keys to the block, made our way through the kitchen and out via the back door into the now inky black night. The small torch we had barely illuminated anything, as we made our way down the two concrete steps to the bunker entrance. We unlocked the massive steel door and made our way into the bunker, shutting and locking the door behind us, as instructed. Switching on lights as we progressed into the underground building, we made our way through each room until we arrived at the emergency lighting room. On our way we had been accompanied by the humming, clicking and whirring noises, as previously described.

As we carried out the checks we spoke very little to each other, and when we did speak, for some strange reason we spoke in whispers. As Don switched on the lights of the emergency lighting room, a most horrendous wailing noise suddenly erupted all around us. It was a terrible groaning sound that filled us both with terror. We turned on our heels and, without switching off any of the lighting, ran in a panic towards the bunker entrance door. There was a great fumbling as we anxiously tried to find the correct key from the bunch, to open the main door. The whole of the time we were running through the block the wailing and groaning sound was all around us. Panic stricken, we managed to open the steel door and, slamming it behind us, locked it and then ran towards the lighted kitchen window. Opening the kitchen door, we rushed in banging the door in our haste.

When we entered the main part of the hut, we found Taffy seated in the armchair reading his book. He looked up at us innocently and said, 'Blimey, what's up with you two?' 'We've seen Eric the ghost', I blurted out. Taffy looked at us with an incredulous grin on his face. 'Come off it', he said. 'Well we haven't seen him really, but we've definitely heard him'. The SP looked at us both and grinning, with what I took to be disbelief, he went back to his book, meanwhile I could still feel my heart pounding in my chest.

Each hour after that, until just after midnight, the corporal seemed to take great delight in advising us that it was time to do our checks. It was with great trepidation that Don and I carried out our duties that night for Queen and country.

At about half-past midnight, Taffy said, 'I'm going to get my head down for a couple of hours, if I was you I would get some shut-eye too'. We needed no second telling, we both pulled chairs together and made makeshift beds. I got very little sleep that night.

The following morning, I awoke to the smell of frying bacon, our policeman friend was up and in the kitchen making himself breakfast. 'You had better get yourself spruced up and get some breakfast' he said, 'The transport will be here in about three-quarters of an hour, to take us back to Warton'. Don and I had a quick cold water wash and set about making some breakfast. After washing the pots and pans, we folded our blankets and sat awaiting the transport.

On arriving back at Warton, I went to bed for a couple of hours and then went down to the NAAFI. There was a group of lads who had been on fire piquet at the various establishments overnight and I joined them after buying a pot of tea and a bun.

There was general chatter about what they had been doing the previous night and, at an appropriate moment I said, 'We had a right experience last night at QQ', I then regaled them with the story of our encounter with Eric the ghost. Suddenly one of the lads said, 'Who were you on with? Taffy?', I said, 'Yes'. The lad looked around with a grin on his face and said to the group collectively, 'He's caught some more with his jape'. I asked him what he meant and he replied, 'What Taffy does is, he sends you into the block and then waits until you are well into the building. He then climbs up the grass bank until he is on top of the block, where there is an air intake tower, about six-foot high. In the side of the tower are wooden louvered slats, to allow air to be sucked into the underground structure. He takes out a couple of the louvers and sticks his head into the tower, and moans and groans down into the ducting that takes the air into the block.

The ducting goes through every room in the building, with vents leading off from the galvanised tubing at intervals of about twenty feet. The ducting amplifies Taffy's voice and that is why the sound seems to come from all around you, he's caught loads of sprogs like that'. Everybody laughed, and I joined them in my embarrassment, joke or not, it was pretty scary at the time.

I can recall other incidents that happened at QQ. On one summer evening, the corporal on duty with us said that he was going to kill a few rats. Just below the Nissen hut there was a narrow stream that meandered along, with banks that undulated, first high on one side of the river and then high on the other. The banks were dotted with holes, which the corporal said were rat-holes. In the hut was a large Jerrycan of petrol which the corporal dragged down to the riverbank, he poured petrol down one of the holes and then, after removing the Jerrycan to a safe distance, struck a match and threw it into the entrance to the rat-hole. There was a low 'WOOMPH' and then a flame came out of the hole for a few seconds and then nothing. Whether he killed any rats or not we never found out. The corporal tired of his game and we went back to enjoying the late evening sunlight.

On another occasion when I was on fire piquet at QQ, the three of us on duty were sat quietly reading when a scraping noise came from behind the stove, at the side of the Nissen hut. All three of us looked up at the same time, and saw a little mouse pop its head out from behind the stove momentarily, and then it disappeared. When we looked behind the stove, we found a very small mouse-hole. We decided to try and catch the mouse. Fetching the dustbin lid from outside the hut, we got a stick and propped the lid up, quite close to the side of the stove. A piece of string was fastened to the bottom of the stick. A quick yank on the string pulled the stick out from under the lid and the lid fell onto the ground. The trap worked well, all we needed was some bait.

From the rations supplied for our night duty, we got some bread and some Cheddar cheese, sprinkling the broken bits under the propped up bin lid. We then sat back and patiently waited for Marmaduke the mouse to appear. Nothing happened for ages and then, just as we were all nodding off, a scratching noise alerted us to our little visitor. He popped his head out from behind the stove and looked around. Slowly he made his way towards the bread and cheese. The corporal tightened his grip on the string and got ready to spring the trap. I was suddenly overcome by the funniness of the situation of a corporal and two airmen of the Queens air force, pitting their wits against a little mouse, and I burst out laughing. The corporal pulled the string far too early and the lid clattered down and Marmaduke made a swift exit behind the stove. The corporal was not amused and hardly spoke to me for the rest of the night shift.

On another occasion at QQ, I was on duty with another 'erk' and a RAF policeman. Just after midnight the SP said, 'I don't think you need to check the block any more, pull a couple of chairs together and get your heads down'. Always being one to obey orders and wishing to please our policeman friend, I did as I was told and so did the other airman. The policeman also pulled two chairs together and then turned the main lights off in the Nissen hut, leaving the kitchen light on. He partly closed the kitchen door and left just enough illumination in the hut for me to make out various objects in the room. I was tired and drifted off into sleep. I awoke to a banging noise and jumped up from the chair, just in time to see the SP, in his pants, vest and socks, but wearing his cap, hurrying to the front door, from whence the banging was coming. He opened the small door, which was set into the large door and the next thing I saw was an officer's cap, as the head on which it rested, bent down to enter the hut. I turned on the main lights and recognised the officer as a Flight Lieutenant who had recently been posted to Longley Lane.

Although the other 'erk' and I had not undressed before retiring, the fact that there were three 'beds' was proof that we had all been asleep. The officer instructed the SP to put on his uniform and then invited him to go outside with him. I was pretty scared and the look on the other airman's face told me that he was scared too. I had heard stories of soldiers being shot for sleeping on duty and wondered what would happen to us. I thought the least we could expect was to be dragged up in front of the CO on a charge. After a few minutes we heard the staff car start up outside and the SP came back into the hut. 'Phew, that was a near one', he said, 'You can normally hear the perimeter fence gate scrape as it opens, but I never heard a thing'. 'It's a good job it was Flight Lieutenant Fortune and not one of the others, he's a decent guy'. That was the last we heard of that, I don't know whether the officer gave the SP a bouncing or not, he never told us, what I do know was that I had kept my slate clean and was very lucky to have done so.

Flight Lieutenant Fortune was involved in another incident that I can remember. We had three police dogs attached to our unit and they resided in kennels at the rear of RAF Longley Lane, in three separate wired off compounds. One of the dogs, Gary, injured his leg and had to be seen by the vet, who ordered that he be kept indoors in a warm environment until his leg was better. It was decided that the dog could use the carpenter/handyman's workshop room at the back of the block and Gary's handler made up a bed for him in the room. The next day, the civilian carpenter/handyman came to work, unaware of the presence of Gary in his workshop. He signed in on entering the block and the policeman on duty neglected to tell him of the situation. The workman made his way to the workshop to collect his toolbox and, seeing a light was on in the room, through the small window in the door, wisely looked through the window. On seeing the dog he did not enter, but went to seek some assistance.

On his way back to the police desk he met Flight Lieutenant Fortune. He told the officer of the situation and Flight Lieutenant Fortune said, 'Don't worry, there's no problem, Gary knows me, I'll get you your toolbox'. The workman followed the officer, who foolishly entered the workshop. He found out to his cost that, whilst he knew Gary, Gary did not know him. Neither did he respect the uniform of an officer, the Flight Lieutenant received a couple of nasty bites and the carpenter/handyman had to await Gary's handler, before he got his toolbox.

7. RAF Longley Lane (3)

(Where I become a skiver)

Exactly six months after I joined the RAF, I got my first recognisable promotion. Every Airman joining the service started out as an Aircraftman 2nd Class. In the trade I was in, successful completion of the trade training course meant an immediate promotion to Aircraftman 1st Class.

I was on duty one day when the Airman relieving me in the Ops. Room said, 'You've to report to the Chiefie's office. The 'Chiefie' was Flight Sergeant Dennis, one of the many Welshman on the unit. When I got to the office, my 'oppo' Chris from Dewsbury was there, along with another lad named Lewis. After a short while the Flight Sergeant called us all in and said, 'All three of you have been promoted to Leading Aircraftman. Your promotion was automatic, however, if you want to get any higher, you have to pass certain tests'. He then asked if any of us had got School Certificates, Chris had, but Lewis and I hadn't and were told we would have to start going to education classes once a week on Thursdays. The Chiefie then said, 'Go to the MT office and see the Corporal and tell him that he must arrange transport to take you to Warton for a casual clothing parade to pick up your insignia'. I was absolutely chuffed. We went to the MT office, as we had been ordered and passed on the Chiefie's message. The Corporal instructed one of the drivers to take us to Warton. The driver folded up the paper he had been reading and, somewhat reluctantly, got out of his chair, pulled his beret out of his lapel and just walked out of the office. We three followed on like Lemmings. We collected our security passes from the Police desk and followed the driver out of the block and into the car park. He walked over to the C.O.'s car, a Standard Vanguard and opened the door, Lewis got in the front passenger seat and Chris and I climbed into the back. We felt like Lords. The driver took off at speed, skidding the back wheels on the cinder-covered car park. The journey to Warton was very fast and a little more comfortable than our normal mode of transport between the two locations.

On arrival at No.1 Site at Warton, after a brief stop at the entrance gate, the driver went straight to the clothing stores. 'I'll be waiting here', he said, 'Don't be long'. We went into the stores and each of was issued in turn with three sets of LAC badges, the insignia consisted of an embroidered two bladed propeller, in light blue, set against a darker blue background. Whilst at the stores, I drew a new pair of socks. We went back to the car and the driver said, 'It doesn't seem worth you lot going back to the block, I'll drop you off at 8 Site'. He drove out of the No. 1. Site gate, turned left and drove down the Lytham road to our domestic site.

As he turned in to the site entrance, the SP on the gate, seeing a staff car immediately lifted the stanchion pole and threw up a salute. I had slipped the new pair of socks over my hands and, as we passed the SP, I threw up my sock-covered left hand in a reply salute. Whether the SP realised what he had done I do not know but we sped into the MT yard, where the driver dropped us off, before driving back in the direction of the main gate. I was full of myself, not only had I been promoted, but I had been saluted by a 'Snowdrop'.

That evening after tea, I couldn't wait to get my 'props' sewn on to my working blue uniform sleeve. I got out my 'housewife', a sort of cotton wallet, which contained, needles, cotton, a hank of air-force blue wool, a card with shirt buttons and some fly-buttons. All Airmen were issued with a 'housewife' on joining up and had to learn how to sew.

I sat on my bed, cross-legged, just like a real tailor, and started sewing one of the insignia patches on to the left sleeve of my working blue jacket. The first attempt was rubbish and the material around the badge was all crumpled. I decided to take the badge off and start again. The second attempt was much better, but, by the time I had done both sleeves, it was time to turn in. I decided to take my other badges home and let my mother or sister sew them on my 'best blue' jacket and overcoat.

The next day, I walked about with my arms sticking out at the front, in an endeavour to let everyone see what an 'old sweat' I was.

The Thursday afternoon education classes at Warton proved to be a right skive, the first of the skives in which I was to become involved. We did lessons on various subjects and it was like being back at school again. English literature, English language, geography, history, current affairs and maths were all covered and I enjoyed the lessons, finding most of the work quite easy. Our teacher was a Warrant Officer and he made all of the subjects quite interesting. We did some psychological tests, which consisted of us individually looking at some inkblots on paper and telling the Warrant Officer what we thought we could see. He then did some word association tests, in which he said a word and you had to say the first word that came into your head, for example, when he said, 'Mother', I said, 'Home'. One of the other lads told me that he had said, 'Father', in reply to the same word. Who was right I don't know, the Warrant Officer simply wrote down your reply on a form. Whatever, I passed my RAF Education Tests Part One and Part Two, which meant that when the time came, I could proceed to RAF Stanmore, to take my trade test for promotion to Senior Aircraftman, that however comes later.

The next skive I got on came about one day in the airmen's mess room at Longley Lane. In the corner of the room was a bookcase, the top part having glass doors, whilst the bottom had wooden doors. Each day, between 1000hrs and 1100hrs a Senior Aircraftman unlocked the bookcase and spent the next hour issuing out library books to any interested airman. I have always been book mad, so I became one of his best customers. One day the SAC said to me, 'Do you fancy running the library?' He then went on to tell me that he was due for demob and said he would like to hand over to someone who was interested. There was no consultation with anyone in authority, I simply took over the keys to the cupboards and started running the library. The SAC had told me that every month a couple of new books would arrive from two book clubs. The new books were chosen by Pilot Officer Cotton and always arrived in his name.

Once Cotton had read them, he would send the books down to the library. Books were loaned out for two weeks and any late books attracted a fine. With the money accumulated from the fines, I purchased second-hand books from a bookshop in Preston, during my lunch break. On one occasion, I saw a well-thumbed copy of 'Lady Chatterley's Lover'. Under the title was the word '*Abridged*'. Anyhow I bought it and it went into the library for a short time but spent most of its time out on loan. One of the lads in Ops 'B' borrowed the book and when it became overdue, I asked him about its return. He told me that Pilot Officer Cotton had seen him reading it and asked where it he obtained it from; he seemed amazed apparently that there were books in the library that had not been first vetted by him. He 'borrowed' the book off the airman and it was never handed back in. The '*Abridged*' version was quite mild at the side of the unexpurgated copy that caused the famous Penguin Books court case some years later. Shamefully, I still have one of the books which belonged to the small Longley Lane library, it is titled, 'The Seventh's Stag Hounds' and is a fictional story about Custer and the American 7th Cavalry.

When I was about 11 years old, my Dad bought a small hand-wound film projector from which we projected black and white cartoon films. We had several films, Mickey Mouse, Donald Duck, etc., and my pals and I spent many a happy hour projecting the films on to the wall or a bed-sheet. When we got fed up of watching them normally, we would go into fits of laughter, winding the films through the projector backwards. I felt the films were funnier in reverse than forwards. Anyhow, one day one of the sergeants came into the mess room and said, 'Has anyone here ever had any experience in using a film projector?'

With tongue in cheek, I said, 'Me sarge'.

'Go with this corporal and he will show you how to operate the station projector'. Skive three. I went as instructed and the corporal introduced me to a magnificent 16mm sound projector, air-cooled and self-lubricating. The projector was used to show trade training films to airmen and to members of the Royal Artillery, who were attached to the unit. Films were ordered from the Army Kinema Corporation in Chester and as well as training films, it was possible to borrow some feature films, these were usually about the Second World War, very often of a propaganda nature. I remember one American film I borrowed, which was about the importance of only giving your name, rank and serial number, if the enemy captured you. It was about an American aircrew who had been shot down and captured by the Germans. Each airman was interrogated individually and the film showed how they contributed to giving a little bit of useful information to his captors, by straying away from the rule of name, rank and serial number. One of the airmen thought that by giving the Germans false information, he was duping them, however, the Germans knew to discount any information freely given and by a process of eliminating the squadron numbers given by the various members of the crew, they arrived at the correct information.

After I had become proficient with the projector, I was called away from my normal job to show films on a fairly regular basis, it was a grand skive.

One of my many leave passes from RAF Longley Lane.

One day I was showing a film about gunnery range finding when the door opened and a sergeant came in. He came and stood by my side at the back of the room and stood watching the film for some time. He then spoke to me in a subdued voice, saying, 'Do you ever get any blue films airman?'

I was very innocent in those days and my answer was, 'No sergeant, we only have black and white or colour'.

The sergeant was amused by my naivety. I felt a right fool when he explained to me what 'blue' films really were. He then went on to tell me a tale about his being a Duty Corporal one night at some air force station. He said he was doing his rounds checking the accommodation huts and was amazed to find all of the huts deserted, until he walked into one hut and was nearly swept back out by the amount of cigarette smoke that came out of the hut door. A 'blue' film was being shown and nearly every 'erk' on the station was in the one hut. Something of a panic ensued and the general cry was, 'Don't report us corporal'. The sergeant said that he had told them he would not report them, on one condition, which was that they start the film again from the beginning. I can well imagine that he was a very popular Duty Corporal that night.

One night on fire piquet, on a request from the others on duty, I moved the projector, with assistance from the others, into the Ops 'B' office. One of the SPs had suggested that, if we projected down into the Ops room we would get a massive picture. Our work was in vain, the picture would not penetrate through the glass windows and we finished up with a smaller picture on the glass window. We then had to cart the projector back down to the training room on the bottom floor.

Throughout the rest of my service I was one of the station projectionists, there being another lad, who was trained up in the job also.

After about three months as a LAC, my name came up to go to RAF Stanmore to take the trade test with a view to me becoming a Senior Aircraftman. Accompanying me on the day of this adventure was LAC Lewis. Other 'erks' who had trodden the same road previously, advised us to book in at the Union Jack Club, a type of hotel for servicemen staying in London. Our colleagues told us that we would have plenty of time to get to Stanmore, from central London, on the day of the trade test.

Lewis and I wended our merry way to the 'smoke' and duly booked in at the Union Jack Club. There were no single or twin rooms available, so we finished up in a dormitory, with about twenty beds. We had arrived in the late afternoon and stowed our kit away in the bedside locker and then we two innocents went out into the fleshpots of central London.

We had a meal in a cheap restaurant and then went round the bright lights. We finished up at Piccadilly Circus and wandered up some of the back streets, as we passed a doorway, a female voice came from the shadows, 'Looking for a good time lads?', well we were but not the type of good time she meant, in any case, I doubt whether we had enough money between us for just one of us to have a 'good time'. Still it was a new experience being propositioned. After wandering around the streets of what I now know was Soho, we made our way wearily back to the Union Jack Club.

When we went in, I was amazed at the number of servicemen and the variety of uniforms we saw. As well as British servicemen, there were soldiers, sailors and airmen from many other countries, The place was packed full. We saw a Canadian soldier who had made up his bed on the top of a grand piano, which graced one of the lounges at the club. We went down to the dormitory, which was below street level. Lying in bed, I could see the images of people walking past on the pavement outside, above and to the back of my bed. The city never quietened down and I got hardly any sleep that night.

Early the following day, we made our way to RAF Stanmore and reported to the guardroom, we were given our instructions and eventually found ourselves in an underground facility, which had been a wartime Operations room. We sat a written test with questions about map reading, and the identification of the types of radar which were in use at that time in the UK. Then came the part I was dreading, and of which our colleagues had warned us, the actual plotting on a map table. I remember that the recorded 'plots' started coming through quite slowly at first and once I had settled down, it was very little different from plotting on our own table at Longley Lane.

The plots then started to speed up and I missed the odd one. Eventually a corporal tapped me on the shoulder and told me to remove my headset and follow him, I was certain that I had failed. We went to a small office where he asked me a few more questions. He then extended his right hand and shook hands with me, saying, 'Congratulations, you've passed your trade test, I am going to recommend you for Senior Aircraftman'. He then took me to a small canteen, where I found Lewis waiting, his face beaming. 'How did you get on', he asked. I told him my good news. Even though I knew from his face the answer, I asked him how he had fared, he told me he had passed also. It was two happy airmen who made their way back to RAF Warton that evening. We arrived back at camp in the late evening after a long day, most of the lads had retired and we were too knackered to impart our good news, it had to wait until the following day.

It seemed ages from us returning from RAF Stanmore, to me receiving official notification of my promotion, once again I could not wait to get my new (three prop) insignia on my arms. I really felt like an old sweat now.

Shortly after my promotion to SAC, I got in on another skive. Skive four involved me working in the Meteorological Office. The flight sergeant came up to me one day and said, 'Airman Voyse, go up to the Met Office and report to SAC Atkinson, he is going on leave in a fortnight and I want you to learn how to do his job'. I duly reported to the Met Office. Brian Atkinson had about three months' seniority over me and had been working in the Met Office for some considerable time. He was a quiet person who never started a conversation on a social basis. He showed me what I needed to know about the job in the Met Office, and, once I became proficient, only spoke to me on the odd occasion and then usually when I had started the conversation. I thought of him as being a lot older than me, because, (a) he wore glasses and they made him look older than he probably was, and, (b) he was engaged to be married. He kept a photograph of his fiancée on the bench in the Met Office.

The job I was trained to do was quite simple really. In the office were three teleprinters, on which came information from various parts of the UK. The information came through in code and it was my job to decipher the code. The teleprinters printed out RAF station identifications, (from where aircraft flew), and then five blocks of five numbers every hour, on the hour. We had a code sheet, which was changed on a regular basis. Out of every block of numbers by using the code sheet, we extracted two numbers from each block. Once we had those two numbers we looked at a chart that carried just about every type of weather condition possible.

Different types of cloud formation were identified as well as the density and height of the cloud and any other features such as, rain, snow, sleet etc. It was from doing the job that I learned what the word 'precipitation' meant. Wind speeds were identified using the Beaufort scale. I eventually finished up with a weather report for every RAF (flying) station in the UK. Armed with the current weather report for the UK, I had to go to the 'Ops B' cabin and display the report on a wall map. Every operational RAF station was shown on the map, being pinpointed by a cup-hook. Onto the cup-hooks I had to hang a series of plaques, which carried the Weather State at the individual airfields. A typical display might read, '5/8ths of cloud at 10,000 feet, surface winds mild to moderate, ice on runway', each separate bit of information being on a plaque that overlapped the next plaque. The controlling officer could see the weather states at the airfields by simply turning his swivel chair and looking to his left at the wall map.

The job was sometimes a little boring, but it had the advantage of largely being an unsupervised job, we rarely got visitors in the Met. Office and so between displaying one lot of information and the next lot coming through, there was an opportunity to read, or play on one of the teleprinters. Once the reports started coming through, the machines had the capability to override whatever you were doing. Sometimes, if we were really bored, we corresponded with unknown, faceless airmen at some location in the country. Simply by typing in a question, or comment, someone, somewhere, would invariably respond. I remember being sat at the bench one day when one of the printers kicked into action. I looked at the script and the following appeared, 'Any WAAF's on this line?' There was a long pause with no response. The unknown airman then started to type a filthy joke complete with obscene language. If there were any female operators, they kept very quiet.

I was supposed to revert back to my normal duties once SAC Atkinson returned from his leave, but I continued to run the library, show films and spend the rest of my time in the Met Office, incredibly no one questioned me about what I was doing.

In the Met. Office, at the rear of the bench which held the teleprinters, there was a hatch which led through to another office. In that office worked a 'Geordie' teleprinter operator, who would often open the hatch door and shout something through. Whatever he said was always a mystery to me, he was a pleasant enough person, but I hadn't a clue what he was talking about most of the time. I used to just laugh and nod my head, I bet he thought I was some sort of idiot.

Former Main Ops bunker at Longley Lane as it is today. (photo: Howard Martin)

It was around this time that I decided to enrol at the Lytham College of Further Education to learn typing. I applied through the unit Admin. Office, filling application forms etc. I don't know whether the RAF paid for my course, or whether I got the course free as a serving serviceman, however, I received instructions and a 'students' bus pass and went off to the enrolment. You can imagine my joy when I found that I was the only male in a class of 40 females. We all were seated in a large classroom, each with a large manual typewriter in front of us. Typing was done to music and the noise of all those typewriters clicking at the same time made a right din. Halfway through the evening there was a break for refreshments and I bought myself a cup of tea and stood there looking at all of the 'talent' and sizing them up in my mind. Groups of girls stood about chattering and giggling, but no one seemed to notice the lonely airman, stood drinking his tea. Suddenly a woman, who I thought to be very ancient, but who might have only been in her late thirties or early forties, came up to me and said, 'Are you at RAF Warton?', 'Yes' I replied. She then said, 'I'm going along the Lytham by-pass on the way home, would you like a lift?' Somewhat embarrassed, I replied, 'Yes please'.

I never used my bus pass again, as the lady picked me up every week opposite the 'No 8 site' gates, and deposited me outside the camp gates after the evening class. Incredibly, the woman worked at the Mayfair restaurant as a cashier in the main restaurant and sat at a raised enclosed desk just past the staircase we had to ascend every day for our lunch. She would wave at me if she saw me in the crowd and I was the butt of some coarse humour from my colleagues. Just my luck, out of all the lovely young girls, I 'clicked' with a mature lady, who, I felt was old enough to be my mother (although she was probably not). Every time she picked me up, she would start the conversation with the same observation, 'You want to be careful crossing that road, I can hardly see you in that dark uniform'.

One of the difficulties I met, taking the course, was the lack of a proper typewriter on which to practise. The only thing I had was one of the teleprinters in the Met Office. The problem was that teleprinters always type one letter behind. Type a letter 'A' and nothing appears on the paper, type a letter 'B' and the 'A' appears. Press down the letter 'C' key and the 'B' is typed on the paper. You can imagine the complications and understand why I dropped behind the rest of the class with my typing skills. Regrettably I did not pass my examination at the end of the course, so did not get any formal typing qualification, however I could type at a speed which gave me satisfaction and has served me well throughout my life.

8. RAF Warton

(A funny sort of social life)

RAF Warton was a massive camp, there must have been at least 11 or 12 sites between the village of Freckleton and Lytham-St Annes, that's including the hospital site, the radar site and the bomb storage site, which had its own rail link with the British Railways main line. The main Lytham road cut through the middle of the camp in a large horseshoe shape. The airfield and landing strip were on the opposite side of the road from our domestic site and the river Ribble ran along the southern boundary of the airfield.

There was not much to do of an evening, after our shift had been completed at Longley Lane. I spent a lot of my time reading. Outside our hut was a wide grass verge and, in the summer groups of airmen lounged about or played games on the grassed area. In winter, the centrally heated huts were quite comfortably warm and it was pleasant to lay on your 'pit' (RAF slang for an airman's bed) and read or listen to the radio. The 'Goon Show' was very popular at that time and on the night of the show, the hut would be full and the radio turned up to maximum volume. I am still a fan of that crazy programme and have several recordings of the various shows. The film 'Dambusters' came out whilst I was in the RAF and the famous 'Dambusters' march by Eric Coates, was regularly played on the radio. One of the lads, who came from Gainsborough, vehemently hated the RAF and all that it stood for, he would run around the huts switching off radios, whenever the 'Dambusters' march came on, to the annoyance of some of the lads.

The NAAFI was always popular. In those days we always seemed to be hungry and it was nothing to down chips and egg, or sausage, around 9 o'clock at night, after having had a hot meal in the cookhouse about three hours earlier. There was a television room in the NAAFI and we would watch programmes on the single BBC channel in black and white. Programmes were often interspersed with 'intervals', either a potters wheel turning boringly round on which there was a piece of pottery that was never completed, or a farmer ploughing a field with his team of shire-horses. It was on that television that a large number of worried airmen, many like me near to our release date, watched the then Prime Minister, Anthony Eden, telling the nation about the Suez crisis in Egypt. More on that episode later.

The 'Astra' cinema was quite a way from '8 site'. If you went out of the main gate, it was a bus ride around the 'U' shaped road. We had a short cut however; if you walked to the top of our road and across a field, there was a hole in the fence from which a well-trodden path led to a bridge, erected by the local council, over a ditch at the side of the road. The journey to the 'Astra' was cut by a half using the hole in the fence. As ours was only a domestic site, no doubt the security risks were not great and the people in authority turned a 'blind eye' to the short cut.

One night, I and a lad named John who was also from Sheffield and one of my bed neighbours, decided to go to the cinema. We used the usual route and, as we were halfway across the field, we heard the shout 'Stop'. We looked to see an SP rushing towards us through the long grass. The SP caught up with us and said, 'Where have you two just come from?' We looked at him gob-smacked and answered that we had come from hut 148. 'Follow me', said the SP. Scared stiff, we followed the SP back through the field and down the camp roads to the guardroom. We entered the guardroom, I could feel my heart pounding in my chest.

'Wait there', said the policeman.

We stood looking at one another, John's face was crimson and from the feeling I had, I was also blushing.

A sergeant came out of a backroom and said 'Sit in that office, pick up those pots of tea and pretend to be drinking out of them'. John and I did as we were instructed, sitting at the table holding up the half-filled pots. Neither of us could understand what was going on.

Suddenly a WRAF girl walked past the door of the room and looked in. We heard her say to the policemen, 'No, that's not them'.

After a few minutes the sergeant came into the room and said, 'Clear off and next time leave by the main gate'. It was two very relieved but angry airmen who walked back up to hut 148. We had had a frightening experience and our proposed night out at the cinema was ruined, it was too late to go to the 'Astra'.

The following day, John and I asked for an audience with the Longley Lane commanding officer. When we saw Squadron Leader Butcher, we poured out our tale of woe and made a complaint against the two policemen. The CO listened carefully to us and then said, 'I'm afraid there's not much I can do about the situation. Whilst everyone is aware of the short cut to the cinema via the hole in the fence, officially you should always enter and leave the site by the main gate. If you had been leaving by the main gate, I may have been able to do something about the actions of the police, but I can't help you in this instance'.

We had to accept what he said, and left his office still disgruntled. We found out later that someone had been seen peeping into the WRAF billets earlier on the evening of our 'arrest'. Whether they caught the culprits, we never found out.

The films at the 'Astra' changed three times a week and the programme operated on a Monday/Tuesday, Wednesday/Thursday and Friday/Saturday basis. The cinema was closed on Sunday. Sometimes, particularly if the picture was boring, it got quite boisterous in the cinema building. I remember one night, in the middle of a quiet part of a film, when most people were engrossed in the plot, a tub of ice cream came flying through the air. The missile hit the cinema screen near to the top and then slowly slid down, for about a yard, before falling on to the narrow stage. For the rest of the film we had to watch the film with a streak of ice cream interfering with the visual image being displayed. The last time I travelled through Freckleton and Warton, the old cinema was still there, but had been converted into a car sales showroom.

On occasions I visited the cinema in St. Anne's-on-Sea, usually accompanied by my mate Ted, or John, the lad from Sheffield who slept in the next bed to me. Sometimes a group of us would traipse down to the cinema and have a wander around the town centre eyeing up the local talent. The girls in the locality seemed to want little to do with servicemen, I think it was a case of 'familiarity breeds contempt', I can't recall any of the lads on our unit having girl friends from the areas around RAF Warton.

A couple of funny incidents occurred on visits into St. Anne's-on- Sea. Ted and I went to the cinema one night. The film was one of those epics that had an interval, which gave the cinema-goers chance to go to the toilet and the cinema owners a chance to sell refreshments to the audience. Anyhow, Ted and I decided to pay a visit to the toilet. When we entered the loo, there was a urinal with enough positions for three persons; a man, in civilian clothing standing in the centre of the urinal. I took up a position to the left whilst Ted stepped up to the right hand side of the urinal. As I started to wee, Ted spoke to me and I looked over to him on my right. When I turned my head, I realised that the man in between Ted and me was none other than our Commanding Officer from Longley Lane, Squadron Leader Butcher. Ted and I were both in uniform, so there was no hiding our identity. As Ted looked at me, he also recognised the CO and the recognition was mutual, as Ted, being in the Admin. Office, regularly did work for the CO. For a minute, I didn't know whether to stand to attention and salute or what to do. Ted being a little more familiar with the CO simply nodded his head and said, 'Evening, Sir!'. We stood at the urinal a little longer than was necessary, as the CO tidied himself up, washed his hands and left the loo. As soon as the door had shut, we both started laughing like idiots. Still it taught me a lesson, even CO's have to answer to the call of nature.

On another occasion a group of us had been to the cinema one very cold night. After the show we had a little time to wait before the Blackpool to Preston via Freckleton bus came along. We all wandered down to beach and soon found ourselves by the side of the pier. The night was freezing cold and our exhaled breaths looked as though we were all smokers. When we got to the water's edge, we were surprised to see that it was frozen. Now that part of the coast is really the very edge of the estuary of the river Ribble so perhaps the salt content of the water was not enough to prevent it from freezing. Anyhow, we tentatively put our feet on to the ice and we were surprised to see that at the very edge, the ice was thick enough to support our weight. We started sliding along the edge of the frozen water, backward and forward, having great fun. Some of the lads got a little more adventurous and went further out. Suddenly there was an ominous cracking sound as one of them fell through the ice. He was up to just above his knees in water and the bottom half of his uniform trousers were soaked through. He crashed his way out of the water and was not the least amused by our laughter. He was shivering all the way back to Warton and was quite embarrassed travelling on the bus with his wet trousers.

During the Second World War, Warton had been an American air force base. It was rumoured that the film star Clark Gable had been stationed there for some time. As stated previously, all the buildings were centrally heated, which contrasted with the usual British type accommodation huts, which normally had a pot-bellied stove set in the centre. Insulated pipes ran along the sides of the camp roads, carrying hot water to the buildings and to the ablution units. There was one ablution unit for every four huts. There were no baths on the camp, only showers and these had been there since the war. Most times the water in the ablutions was warm, it was never hot. Very often it was tepid, it depended very much on the time of the day and the outside temperature.

You did not have to be prudish as, there was only a half canvas curtain in each of the four shower units in each block. My friends and colleagues had a very warped sense of humour, as often you would be halfway through a shower, when either one or a couple of fire-buckets of freezing cold water would come flying over the top of the short canvas screen. It was a real breath-taker and there was no escape, even if you saw the miscreants approaching with their weapons of terror. It was a give and take situation, I just remembered who had done it to me and marked them down for a reprisal at some later date. It was bad enough during the summer, in winter it was positively cruel. At least you knew when you had had a shower, if you received a visit from 'friends'.

'Streaking', is thought to be a relatively new phenomenon, however, I think it was invented at RAF Warton. Some of the 'erks' on our unit thought it was funny to 'steal' your clothes, including your towel, whilst you were enjoying a shower. You completed your shower, congratulating yourself for not being drenched in cold water, only to find that, when you pulled the shower curtain back, your belongings had been kindly returned to the hut by a helpful 'friend'. It was quite a common sight, at any time of the year, to see a totally naked airman, running back to the billet, with his tackle blowing in the wind. The funny thing was that everybody took it as a joke and there was no nastiness or fighting.

Another joke that was played regularly, was the making of 'French' beds, for those airmen who had been out drinking and returned to the billet after lights out. Usually, if people were going out for the night, they made their beds up so that they could just climb straight in after a night' boozing. We used to wait until they had gone out and then we would carefully strip back the bedding and fold back the bottom sheet so that there was a fold in the middle of the bed, we would then fold the top of the sheet over the blankets and it always appeared as though everything was in order. The unfortunate airman at the receiving end of the joke would arrive back in the hut, undress in the dark and then try to climb into bed. Unfortunately, having put his feet under the covers, the airman would only be able to get his feet halfway down the bed. I remember one airman, who was 'three sheets to the wind', bemoaning the fact that he couldn't get into bed. 'I keep getting into the wrong sheets' he kept saying. The poor lad spent the night in the foetal position, with his knees tucked under his chin.

Another prank played was to get a sheet of newspaper and pin one side to the top of someone's locker and the other side to the top of the door. The door was then closed to make a fold in the newspaper. We would then fill up the centre of the newspaper with all the rubbish we could find. The unsuspecting airman would come into the hut in the dark and having taken his clothes off, would then open the locker door, to put away his clothes. As he opened the door, the centrepiece of the newspaper would rip open and the contents placed in the middle would cascade down on the unfortunate 'erk'. Some wild cursing would follow and we would be holding back our laughs, pretending to be asleep. I think everyone in our hut fell for that one at some time or other.

On some summer nights we would spread a blanket on the grass verge outside the hut and bask in the evening sun reading or playing cards, etc.

Soldiers of the Royal Artillery occupied the very last two huts on our camp road. They were attached to the CFP, working as spotters for gun defended areas. This was a throw back from the war when the spotters would warn artillery units of the location of RAF aircraft who were flying in the locality of gun defended areas. I understand that, despite the setting up of such spotter units, a number of RAF aircraft were downed by 'friendly' fire.

One of the army lads was a Lance Bombardier, in other words he had a single stripe on both arms of his uniform jackets. This particular lad was a regular and he had a very smart dress uniform. Every Friday night he would go out in his dress uniform, which consisted of a dark blue jacket and trousers. The trousers had a broad red stripe down them, which matched the red banding on the uniform cap. Frankly, with his bulled boots and white webbing belt, the lad looked extremely smart. However, on fine evenings, he was obliged to pass by groups of National Service type airmen. You could always tell when he was on his way, as whistling would start from the top of the road, which can only be described as, DEE DA DEE DUM, DEE DA DEE, DIDDLE DE DUM, DIDDLE DE DUM, the whistle being taken up all the way down the road. It was all very cruel, the Lance Bombardier would run the gauntlet red faced and always appeared to be cursing at the 'erks', although he never actually said anything. Really, he was either very brave, or thick-skinned. What his luck was with the local ladies I do not know, I never knew where he was off to on a Friday evening.

The American air force left a terrible legacy, as, during the war, a fully loaded bomber crashed on to the Freckleton village school, killing the crew and wiping out a generation of young children and their teachers. In the churchyard at Freckleton there is a memorial which bears witness to this tragic event of many years ago.

As we were an operational unit and because there were a number of auxiliary air force flying squadrons active in our sector, we worked on Saturdays and Sundays. For the purpose of 36 hour passes, our 'weekend' was Monday evening, after stand down, to Wednesday lunchtime. Our passes were issued between the hours of 1730 on the Monday, and 1300 on the Wednesday, when we were supposed to report back for an afternoon of sports. Very few of us reported back for the sports afternoon. For example, the group of people I travelled back to camp with, always caught the 1930hrs train from Sheffield (Victoria) to Manchester (Piccadilly). In other words, every week on a Wednesday when we caught the train at Sheffield, we were already 6½ hours late. The worst part of the journey was crossing central Manchester. Piccadilly was the haunt of the dreaded 'Redcaps' and we very often had to scuttle down side streets and lanes when we saw Military Police approaching. In those servicemen in uniform were common sights on the streets of the UK. Large cities like Manchester were always patrolled in the evenings by Military Police units, both on foot and mobile, usually in open top jeeps. Like the RAF police, they wore white webbing belts and a single over the shoulder strap, with red bands on their left arm bearing the letters 'MP'. As they were inevitably tall, they could be spotted from a distance, which was useful. Considering the number of times we ran the gauntlet across Manchester City centre, luckily my group was only challenged once. Two corporals stopped us and asked us where we were making for, collectively we said Preston. I was looking at one of the MP's boots, in which I could almost see my face, when he suddenly directed his attention on me personally. 'What are you grinning at airman?' he asked. 'Nothing corporal' I replied, I felt distinctively uncomfortable, expecting at any time for the MPs to ask us for our passes. Suddenly the immaculate pair spotted another RAF bod, a corporal believe it or not, who was strolling along with the front of his greatcoat wide open. The MPs thankfully forgot about us and made their way over to the offending airman, we took the opportunity to 'exit stage left', as they say in the acting profession.

One of the lads we used to meet on the Sheffield to Manchester train, was a guy who hailed from Gainsborough in Lincolnshire. This particular lad hated the air force and made it well known, (he was the one who went around turning off the radios, if the 'Dambuster's March' came on). One night, we Sheffielders boarded the train at the Victoria Station and found that our Gainsborough friend was missing. We later found he had missed his train in his hometown. By missing the train he had quite an adventure. He caught the next train, which was around one hour later. This meant that he had to cross Piccadilly in Manchester by himself, which was always a bit more dodgy than walking across the city centre with a group. As luck would have it, two army 'Redcaps' stopped him, and asked to see his leave pass. By this time it was about 2130hrs and he was about 8½ hours adrift. The 'Redcaps' arrested him and took him to an army depot, where they started to look up RAF Longley Lane, in their directory of RAF stations. Being a classified unit at that time, the unit was not listed and the army bods started to get a little suspicious. Our friend told them to contact the RAF police at No. 8 site at Warton and ask to be put through to Longley Lane. Eventually the MP's rang Warton and were duly put through to the duty officer at the SOC. Luckily for the detained airman, the duty officer was Flight Lieutenant Fortune who apparently gave the MP's a dressing down for delaying one of his men and told them to provide him with transport back to Warton. Our Gainsborough friend came back in style in the back of an army jeep and was full of himself when he told us his adventurous tale. The next day however, he found himself on a charge for missing the sports afternoon and for being absent without leave. Although the RAF punished him, it was nice to know that Flight Lieutenant Fortune stood by him when the 'chips' appeared to be down.

Our little group of travellers experienced another close shave one night as we were leaving Preston station. As we got to the barrier, where the ticket collector was doing his bit, two RAF policemen confronted us. They were stopping every airman that came through the ticket barrier. I was one of the first of our group to have to pass them. One of the SPs asked me if I was from RAF Kirkham, Weeton or Warton. Fearing the worst I said, 'Warton'. With a casual flick of his thumb, the policeman waved me past him. I breathed a big sigh of relief. Our group walked out of the station without talking and collectively, on reaching the top of the station approach road, started jabbering and congratulating ourselves on another near miss. What the SPs were looking for, we never found out, we were just happy that they had not asked to inspect our out of time leave passes.

Going the other way was much more interesting, obviously, because I was going home, but also because I always hitchhiked on the homeward journey. Each week it was the same. Those thumbing it dropped off the RAF transport at the Fulwood crossroads in Preston. Groups of airmen stood at the crossroads, waving their thumbs at oncoming vehicles. It was surprising how quickly we were all picked up from that location on the A6. I always travelled with the same lad, Derek from Barnsley. His claim to fame was, that he had won a 'belching' competition, which we held one evening in the back of a lorry, when in the Blackpool lights traffic in Preston, whilst we were trying to get back to Warton one evening. Derek had worked on the railway prior to his National Service and he was a decent sort of a guy. We always felt more comfortable hitchhiking as a twosome. We always stayed together until we reached the Flouch crossroads, on the Yorkshire side of the Woodhead pass, which crossed the Pennines. Depending on where the vehicle was going in which we were travelling, either Derek or I alighted at the Flouch crossroads, where the road went straight on to Barnsley or you took the right turn to Sheffield. We had some rare lifts over the Pennines, in a multitude of differing vehicles. Cars were obviously the favourite, but, in those days, long before the M62 was even thought of, hundreds of lorries crossed the Woodhead pass daily.

On one occasion a brewery lorry picked us up. It was a cold night and Derek and I were glad of the lift. It was warm but noisy in the lorry cab and there was a large black dog lying on the engine cover, which was inside the cab and covered by a quilted material. All over the floor of the cab on the passenger side were bottles of beer, which rolled about as the lorry drove along. We could hardly see the driver, but he was a friendly guy, who shouted all sorts of questions to us as he drove along. He passed a bottle opener to Derek, who was sitting next to the engine cover (and the dog), and invited us to have a bottle of beer if we wanted, we both declined his generous offer. I was crushed up against the cab door, as Derek and I were sharing a seat that was meant for one. The lorry climbed slowly up from Tintwhistle to the top of the Woodhead pass. Just before the summit, the lorry driver turned his vehicle into a lay-by. It was pitch black outside. Stopping the lorry engine, the driver opened his door saying, ' I shan't be long, I'm just taking the dog for a walk, get yourselves a drink if you want'. With that, he dropped out of the cab and out of sight, the dog, who obviously knew what to expect, followed him out of the vehicle. The cab door was slammed and Derek and I sat there, crushed up to one another in the dark cab, listening to the hot engine clicking beneath the cover, as it cooled down. The vehicle's lights were on, but the instrument lights were very dim and gave off very little light. The lorry sidelights gave an eerie glow outside, but we could see nothing. The driver was gone ages and both Derek and I were getting quite apprehensive.

We discussed what could have happened to him and we wondered what we would do if the driver failed to return. After some extensive time, the lorry door opened and the dog's head appeared as the driver lifted him into the cab. It had a sniff at Derek before lying down on the engine cover. The driver climbed in and slammed the cab door, he shouted, as though the engine was running, 'By, its bloody cold out there', he shuddered and hunched his shoulders and started up the lorry. The vehicle climbed slowly out of the lay-by and onwards up to the top of the pass. Our adventures were not over yet however. As the lorry went over the top of the summit, it started to speed up. Suddenly the driver knocked the gearstick into neutral and the vehicle started to pick up speed. Derek and I were hanging on for grim death, I was gripping the window winder on the door whilst Derek was gripping my shoulder, as he had his arm around the back of the seat. Having travelled over the Woodhead pass in daylight, we were aware of the steep drops down the side of the road. At that time there were no crash barriers, just black and white striped posts with reflectors fitted to the top. When we got to the Flouch crossroads, the lorry driver turned his vehicle into the car park of the Flouch Inn and said he was stopping for a short while. We asked where he was going, to which he replied, 'Sheffield'. Derek said, 'Oh, I'll get out here then, I'm going to Barnsley'. I decided to hedge my bets and I said I was going to Barnsley also. We both left the vehicle and walked down towards the Flouch Inn. As we walked away from the lorry, we heard a hissing noise and when we looked back we saw the driver pouring water from a canister on to the hot wheel of the lorry. The man was obviously a tile short of a full roof. I waited until the lorry drove off and the walked across to the Sheffield road, where I thumbed a more civilised lift. Derek in the meantime had got into a vehicle, which had stopped for him and had then disappeared into the darkness of the Barnsley Road.

One day a large furniture van stopped for us. There were three men in the cab, all wearing white aprons over their other clothes. The one nearest the window, on the pavement side, slid the window down and asked us where we were going. I said, 'Sheffield'. The man said, 'We're going to Crosspool, in Sheffield, do you want a lift'. We said yes but wondered where we were to sit, the cab being full. The man we had spoken to, opened the door and jumped out. 'Come round the back', he said. We followed him to the back of the vehicle and he opened the large doors and dropped the tailgate down. 'Get sat in them armchairs', he said, 'you'll be comfortable enough, I'll turn the interior light on'. With that, he closed up the doors and we sat in the dark for a few moments. I heard the cab door slam and them a light came on over the doors and another at the front of the vehicle, giving some modicum of light. It was a strange journey and at first we were a bit apprehensive, nevertheless the armchairs were quite comfortable. There was a piano strapped to the side of the vehicle and Derek lifted the front at one point and had a short play whilst standing up, swaying with the vehicle's movement. Eventually, after what seemed an age, the van stopped and we heard the cab doors bang. The back doors opened and we found we were parked on a road of semi-detached houses. 'If you want to give us a lift, we'll drop you in the centre of Sheffield', said the driver of the vehicle. So Derek and I spent the next half-hour unloading and carrying furniture into the house to which the delivery was being made. I don't know what the woman at the house thought when she saw two young men, in full RAF uniform, carrying chairs and other items into her house. After we had made the delivery, Derek and I climbed back into the rear of the van, this time having to stand holding the slats, which ran, down the side of the van interior. It was not a comfortable journey and we were glad when the van stopped and we were dropped in the centre of Sheffield. When I told my mum I had been delivering furniture on the way home, she thought I was joking.

On another occasion, we were at Hyde, a small town on the edge of Manchester. We were near to some traffic lights and waving our thumbs at anything travelling in an easterly direction. Suddenly a brand new Ford Consul stopped. The driver leaned over and said, 'I'm going to Sheffield, is that any good to you?', without appearing too hasty, we both dived into the rear passenger seats saying, 'Yes please' as we entered the car. We drove in luxury all the way to Bradway, a suburb of Sheffield, on that occasion, we went over the notorious Snake Pass. The car driver turned out to be the Managing Director of a company named Brook Shaws, the main Ford Dealer at that time in

Sheffield. He dropped us at the Bradway golf club and we caught the bus into Sheffield, I got off the about half a mile from my home, whilst Derek travelled into the City terminus and caught the Barnsley bus home. We didn't get many lifts home like that one.

One night, I had left Derek at the Flouch crossroads, he was in luck that night as the lift was going into Barnsley. As I stood at the junction of the Sheffield road, I saw a large American air force lorry, coming down towards Flouch. It turned into the Sheffield road and immediately the brakes went on heavily and the lorry shuddered to a stop. A head covered by a floppy denim hat appeared out of the window way above the kerb. 'Hi, you looking for a lift?', said the head. I shouted, 'Yes please'. The vehicle being a left-hand drive, I had to go out into the middle of the road to start climbing up into the massive cab. Using the grab handles I climbed up the steps and into the large vehicle. The driver was very friendly and was asking me all sorts of questions about the RAF on the way into Sheffield.

It was summer and a sunny evening and as we progressed along the Queen's highway, we kept passing young ladies who were out for an evening stroll. As we passed each of the girls, the American driver reached up into the roof of the cab and pulled down on a cord, which was stretched across the cab roof. The vehicle was fitted with air horns and the cord activated the horns. The driver was having great fun as the sound invariably made the girls jump and sometimes scream. It was a fun ride and I was sorry to leave him when we reached the city centre in Sheffield. I never found out where he was going, or where he had come from, but he was a real friendly guy.

Standing at the Fulwood crossroads one evening, I saw a vehicle coming towards us with the words 'Hallam Steel' emblazoned across the front of the lorry. That was the name of a large steel firm in Sheffield and I was pleased when the lorry stopped. I soon regretted getting the lift though, as the heavily laden vehicle took 5½ hours to get to Sheffield. I thought I was never going to get home.

One day, one of the lads brought a bicycle back to camp that was fitted with an engine in the back wheel, it was called a 'Cyclemaster'. We all took it in turns to drive the thing round the camp roads. I had a go, but found that I couldn't stop the thing, I did two circuits of the road around our huts, eventually having to drive onto the grass and fall off to stop the thing.

Finally, in this chapter about my social life in the RAF. Our evenings in the summer were often affected by late night flying. A team of airmen had to stay behind on what was termed as 'night binds'. Depending on what the weather was like, flying could go on into the early hours of the morning and we often stood down at well after midnight. One funny incident occurred when we were working a night bind. We stood down at about 0145hrs.

The duty corporal rang the cookhouse and ordered a late meal for sixteen airmen. When we were on night binds we always had packed meals delivered to the unit, but, we were always hungry when the shift was over, so even in the middle of the night a meal was usually welcomed by some of us. Others simply wanted to get to bed. We got back to Warton at about 0230hrs and the transport dropped us at the door of the cookhouse. When we went in, we found that the duty cook had misheard our corporal and had cooked a meal for sixty airmen.

There were piles of 'bangers' and 'mash' and we all made pigs of ourselves. Being tired we were very giggly and thought everything was funny. Seeing the large number of thick pork sausages put us into fits of laughter, the cook didn't see the funny side of it. We decided to take some sausage sandwiches back for our mates, who were in the middle of their beauty sleep. You can imagine the reaction I got, when I woke 'Taffy', my other bed neighbour, with a, by now, cold pork sausage sandwich at around half-past three in the morning. He wasn't best pleased, he had to get up the next morning, whilst the other late night operatives and I had got the morning off.

One of the things most of us used to do on entering our hut when we got back to Warton of an evening was to run and dive onto our beds. One evening, I came 'unstuck' following this trend. I ran into the hut and dived onto my 'pit' (RAF slang for bed). As my full weight hit the bed, the top end of the bed collapsed and the iron head of the bed crashed down, trapping me between it and the mattress. I couldn't get up and initially, my mates failed to come to my assistance as they stood about laughing. The metal joints, which connected the bed head to the frame of the bed, had snapped off on both sides. I spent the next couple of hours searching through the old disused Nissen huts, looking for a spare head section for my bed; luckily I found one.

Every so often we were paid what was referred to as 'credits', it was usually an amount of money which had been set aside from our pay to utilise on replacement clothing and other equipment. On the complicated sheet which accompanied the payment of credits, was always an item marked '*Barrack Room Damages*'. In the whole of my service, the only damage I did, apart from to a stovepipe at West Kirby (which we repaired), was to that head section of my bed. We all considered 'credits' to be a fiddle.

All in all, we had a fairly decent social life, we didn't do a lot of drinking, mostly we went to the cinema, or played games on the grass outside the huts. Often, being Lancashire, rain stopped play, and we either stayed in reading or went to the NAAFI to watch television.

9. RAF Turnhouse & RAF Hooton Park

(An Erk Abroad)

The North Atlantic Treaty Organisation (NATO) decided to have a military exercise during 1955. The exercise, named 'Lionheart', was supposed to simulate an attack by the Eastern Bloc, 'Warsaw Pact' forces on various parts of the member countries of NATO.

One of our Flight sergeants gave us a talk on the projected exercise, during which members of the auxiliary air force would man Longley Lane, with just a token number of the permanent staff of the unit. All other members of staff would be posted out to three locations, Germany, Cyprus, and Scotland. A notice was put up in the airmen's mess and we were asked to append our names on to the three sheets carrying the three country names. The result was that, the sheet headed Germany was nearly full, whilst just a few 'Jocks' had put their names down for Scotland, whilst nobody seemed interested in going to Cyprus. This wasn't all that surprising, considering that British servicemen were being injured and killed by the troubles between the Greeks and Turks on that troubled isle.

It was obvious that there would be some intervention from above and, sure enough, when we were informed of our final destination, our numbers had been equally shared out between the three locations. I had selected Germany and finished up with the contingent destined to go to Scotland and the Caledonian Sector of Fighter Command. A few of the lucky ones got their wish and received the posting to Germany, whilst there were others who were cursing their luck because they had been selected for the Cyprus posting.

With the two overseas postings, some of my colleagues were getting their first opportunity to fly with the RAF. We, who had drawn the Scotland straw, were destined to travel by train from Preston to 'Auld Reekie' (Edinburgh).

When the day of travel arrived, we were transported to Preston station and carrying our kit boarded a special carriage, which had been attached to the London to Glasgow train. The RAF had looked after us, because as well as our kit, we were all lumbered with a large brown paper bag, which had been handed to us as we boarded the transport at RAF Warton. We settled into the compartments of the special carriage, eight to a compartment that was designed really to carry six, with swivel arms separating each seat. Anyhow we had to lift the arms in order to accommodate the extra two in each compartment. I managed to get a window seat, which wasn't too bad, as I had a corner to settle into for the long journey north. The lads sitting in the centre of the seat were not so lucky, having to lean on each other when they got tired of sitting up straight.

The train left Preston and passed through the Lancashire countryside and on into what was then Westmoreland. As we travelled into the Lake District, most of us cracked open our packed lunches. There were four rounds of bread and meat, cut into four sandwiches, an apple, a small packet of biscuits and strangely, a screwed up piece of paper, which contained a mixture of tea and sugar. Where we were supposed to get water from to make the tea was a mystery, as was the obtaining of milk supplies. Luckily a British Railways person came round with a trolley on which there was an urn of what was supposed to be tea. Anyhow, it was warm and wet and helped us to get down the 'doorstep' sandwiches, thoughtfully supplied by our colleagues in the catering division of the Air Force. Many a sandwich was seen being hurled from the train and the unusable makings of tea often followed.

We arrived at a railway station and saw the signs, 'CARSTAIRS', prominently displayed at different points on the platform. Just as we were arriving at the station, the guard came through the carriage. He announced that we would have a twenty minute stop, and, if we wished to get off and stretch our legs, or buy something from the station refreshment facility, we could do so. When the train stopped, many of the lads baled out and headed for the refreshment room. I stayed on the train, fearful of losing my comfortable corner seat. I asked one of my colleagues to bring me a 'Kit-Kat' biscuit and a bottle of 'pop'. As I sat looking through the window, I saw a small tank engine go up the line at the side of us, towards the rear of our train. After a short while, there was the feel of something bumping gently into the back of our carriage and clanking noises.

Suddenly our carriage started to move off in the direction from which we had arrived. I stood up and stuck my head through the small sliding window, at the top of the main one. The small engine pulled our carriage away from the main part of the train and into a siding. From the carriage we had a good view of the station platform. Suddenly the guard raised his arm and waved a green flag, at the same time blasting on his whistle, he then stepped into the inward opening door of the guard's van and stood with his head sticking out as the main part of the train started to move.

The doors of the refreshment room flew open and a stream of airmen came running out, looking in amazement as the train picked up speed. A couple of airmen ran down the platform, waving their arms at the rear of the train as it disappeared out of the station. I then saw a railwayman talking to some of the obviously panicking airmen and pointing in the direction of where our carriage was parked. Shortly afterwards another train pulled into the station, which we found out later was from Glasgow and destined for Edinburgh. The fussy little tank engine towed our carriage through the station and then crossed some points, before changing direction and pushing us up to the rear of the Glasgow to Edinburgh train. When our mates re-boarded, those of us who had stayed in the carriage, pulled their legs something rotten. They were not amused in the least by our 'ragging'.

When we arrived at Waverley Street station in Edinburgh, we all decamped from the train on to the station platform, where we stood in an unruly group with our kit awaiting instructions. The citizens of Edinburgh must have wondered what had arrived in their fair city, as there were many phrases in pseudo Scottish accents being bandied about. 'Och aye the noo', and, 'It's a braw brict moonlit noo the noo' was heard being shouted. Someone called out to me, 'Ar ye alreet MacVoyse', to which I replied 'Och aye'. Eventually our NCOs got us in to some semblance of order and we marched off the station.

Outside there were a number of RAF vehicles lined up. We climbed on board and after a short while the convoy moved off up into Princes Street where I got my first view of an Edinburgh tramcar, resplendent in maroon and white. The convoy made its way out of the city centre and eventually we turned into the entrance gates of RAF Turnhouse. Even then the airfield was being used as the airport for the city of Edinburgh. I got my first close up view of a civilian passenger aircraft, as there was a turbo-prop Britannia standing with a mobile staircase pushed up to the open door of the aeroplane. I could see into the plane through the open door and saw a couple of the cabin crew just inside the door. Whether the plane had just arrived, or was waiting to take passengers on board, I do not know, but I was very interested. Our transport dropped us quite near to some very old huts and as we alighted, a sergeant with a clipboard told us which hut to go to. The interior of the hut we entered was very shabby and I was surprised to see that the beds were the double bunk variety. Even more surprising was that, at the bottom of the hut were a number of American airmen laid or sitting about, they all appeared to be sergeants.

I threw my kit onto one of the lower bunks and sat on the edge of the bed taking in the surroundings. Our American friends turned out to be part of the crew of a B29 'Superfortress', which we saw later, parked by one of the hangars. The Americans said 'Hi' to us, but that was the full extent of our fraternisation, they kept pretty much to themselves whilst they were in the hut.

One of the permanent staff of Turnhouse came to show us where the cookhouse was situated and we went and had an enjoyable meal, we were all hungry after our long journey.

Before turning in for the night, I visited the ablutions, which again were very ancient. When I went into one of the toilets, there was a nearly life-size drawing of a nude female on the cork partition wall. Someone who was gifted must have done the drawing, as it looked quite lifelike. The drawing had been defaced however in the private parts region, where a hole had been made in the partition in that very part of the drawing.

The next day after reveille, we had breakfast and then boarded transport for the Caledonian Sector Operations Centre at RAF Barnton Quarry.

We travelled some fair distance from Turnhouse and eventually turned off the main road and into a very narrow road, surrounded by forest. After a short while we pulled onto a large tarmac covered area and stopped. As we alighted from the transport, we saw to the left a perimeter fence and a gate, behind which there was several concrete buildings. The ground behind rose up steeply and to the rear of the buildings was the rock-face of the quarry. To the right, at the other side of the tarmac area, the ground dropped away at an alarming angle, down into the forest.

We were all told to have our Longley Lane security passes at the ready and, in groups of about ten, accompanied by a member of the local staff, we were taken into one of the surface buildings. Inside there was a long counter behind which were a couple of RAF policemen. To the left of the counter was a pair of double doors and, after handing in our security passes, we were told to wait by the doors. Eventually our guide pushed open the double doors and said, 'Follow me'. We followed through the doors and immediately the floor started to drop away. We had entered a sloping tunnel that went down for about one hundred yards and must have dropped about fifty feet.

The paving stones in the tunnel had rubber inserts to stop people from slipping down the slope. At the bottom of the slope we found ourselves on the upper floor of an underground three-storey building, it was like something out of a James Bond movie. There was a lift that went down to the very bottom of the complex but we were taken down the stairs. We were amazed, we had thought that Longley Lane was something special but this place was like something out of the future. On the second floor we were able to see into the Operations room where our Caledonian counterparts were busily plotting away. I was surprised to see that, as well as RAF personnel, there were some Canadian and Norwegian officers on duty.

Whilst at Barnton Quarry I never got selected for any plotting duties, but was involved in quite a number of other activities.

Members of our party were issued with either rifles or Sten guns complete with clips of blank ammunition. I was given a

Sten gun. I had not had a hold of one of these weapons since we had been trained on stripping and re-assembling them at basic training. I had never fired one but had 'cocked' the gun and the pressed the trigger. On the Sten there was a powerful spring which could be seen through the side of the gun and went with a right crack when one pulled the trigger.

We were put on guard duties, and I was put outside the perimeter fence with the instruction to patrol left from the main gate up the hill to where the fence took a sharp left turn, climbing further up the side of the quarry. One of my mates had to patrol from the corner further up the hill to another designated point, where the next airman took over. This situation went on the whole of the way round the fence. As the whole of the area was surrounded by forest, the job of patrolling along the side of the fence was pretty scary and somewhat dangerous at night-time. It was surprising how one's eyes adjusted to the dark.

Two silly things happened whilst I was engaged on patrol duties outside Barnton Quarry. The first one was that I scared my mate, who I was supposed to meet at the corner of the fence. I got up to the corner and could hear my oppo coming down towards the corner. I cocked my Sten gun and crouched down by the perimeter fence. As my mate arrived at the corner, I squeezed the trigger, the noise of the blank going off was louder than I had anticipated and made me jump; my mate, however, fairly did a cartwheel. He went absolutely barmy at me, calling me all names under the sun (or moon at that time of the night).

The second incident happened a few nights later. I had seen a young officer whose peaked cap I took a real fancy to. It was swept up somewhat like the hats worn by the German officers during the war and I thought it was the 'bee's knees'. On the occasion about which I write, I was making my way down from the corner of the perimeter fence, in the direction of the main gate when I saw the silhouette of two persons coming towards me. One of the persons was definitely the aforesaid young officer, as I recognised his distinctive hat. Thrusting my Sten gun forward I prepared to challenge them, as taught, but, like an idiot, knowing that at least one of them was an officer, said, 'Halt, who goes there, SIR!' As soon as I had said it I knew I was wrong. The officer didn't miss out on the silly mistake and took me to task over the challenge I had made.

On the nights when we were on duty, our rest periods were spent in a room into which had been put about forty canvas camp beds. The beds were made up by sliding two long rods through the folded edge of the canvas and the slotting four 'W' shaped pieces underneath, to tauten the canvas and act as legs. Actually they were not too bad to sleep on. We did not undress but simply covered ourselves with a single wool blanket. The shifts were arranged so that you got about four hours kip before having to go out on patrol again.

On one of the nights, we were half way through our rest period and a group of others were in the process of going out to relieve those currently on patrol. I was lying on my bed half-asleep when I heard one of the Longley Lane lads say, 'Are you asleep Brummie?', the reply came back, 'No, we'll get no sleep until these noisy bastards have gone out'. The next minute Brummie was dragged out of his camp bed, by one of the Scottish contingent and he received a 'bunch of fives' right in the face. I pretended to be asleep but was aware of the scuffling which was going on around me as several airmen from the two units exchanged blows. The trouble ceased as some one came in and ordered the Scots lads out on duty.

The fence patrol became a bit of a bind and when one night I heard a lad asking, 'Does anyone want to swap a patrol for a telephone outpost?', like an idiot I volunteered. When we next went on duty, the lad I had swapped went to do my patrol, whilst I accompanied a group of airmen, being taken by an officer and a Territorial Army sergeant through the forest to various points, where particular airmen took up positions vacated by relieved airmen. Eventually there was only the officer, sergeant and me left floundering our way through the dark forest.

At one point the officer said, 'Be careful down this bank, there's some wires!' The next minute the officer disappeared down the bank as he obviously tripped over something or other. Eventually we arrived at a spot and the officer said, 'I think it's around here somewhere. Suddenly out of a clump of bushes an airman emerged and challenged us; this was the erk I was to relieve.

The officer told me to use the field telephone every quarter of an hour and report whether everything in the area was all right. My area was designated 'A' sector. He waved me into the bushes and I bent down and entered the sheltered area under the bushes, there I found a metal 'Jerrycan' and a field telephone in a wooden box. I sat on the Jerrycan and nursed my Sten gun. As the officer, sergeant and the airman made their way back to Barnton Quarry, I could hear them for ages. I thought, if this had been the real thing, they would not have got far. It's surprising how far one can hear when it is totally quiet.

Once on my own I felt very scared, I fancied I could hear all sorts of noises around me. I was distinctly uncomfortable. Time seemed to pass very slowly. I kept looking at the illuminated figures and fingers on my watch and timed myself to the first time I would be using the telephone. Exactly quarter of an hour after my escort had left I picked up the field telephone. Unlike a normal phone, there was no dialling tone. I felt for the winding handle on the side of the box and turned it very slowly, afraid of making a noise; nothing happened. I grabbed the handle again and this time gave the handle a frantic turn, a whirring noise emitted from the box, which I thought would be heard for miles. Suddenly a voice came over the line, 'Control here, go ahead'. I whispered, '"A" sector, nothing to report'. The voice said again, 'Control here caller, go ahead'. Speaking a little louder I said, ' 'A' sector nothing to report. Thankfully the voice at the other end said, 'Roger 'A' sector, out', and the line went dead. And so my first stint at the telephone outpost passed, with me ringing in every quarter of an hour. I was truly RELIEVED, when my relief arrived after four long hours. A couple of nights later, I was on my own at my telephone outpost, still uncomfortable and kicking myself for being foolish enough to swap my duty. During this period of duty I was concerned because of the definite sounds of activity that was going on around me in the forest, something was really astir. In the distance I could hear explosions (no doubt Thunderflashes) and the crack of weapons being fired. I found out later that Barnton Quarry was under attack from the RAF Regiment (the Rock Apes, as they were known).

I picked my field telephone up at the designated time and turned the handle, the usual whirring sound came from the box, but the line was dead. I turned the handle again frantically, nothing! and again, nothing!. After trying a dozen times, it slowly dawned on me that I had a problem, the phone was not working, my wire had been cut somewhere. I sat still for a considerable period pondering my fate, what did I do now? I knew there was no way that I would find my way back up through the forest back to Barnton Quarry. In any case it was obvious that there was some sort of attack being carried out and I didn't fancy being on the wrong end of a Thunderflash, or being taken prisoner by some mad RAF Regiment bod.

Taking my Sten gun, I abandoned my, now useless, field telephone and the Jerrycan and made my way out of the clump of bushes. Looking down through the forest, I could see some orange coloured street lighting, I decided to make my way towards this vestige of civilisation.

For the next half-an-hour or so, I walked, stumbled, fell my way though the forest undergrowth. Bramble bushes tripped me up, I caught myself on gorse bushes, but I progressed ever nearer the street lighting. I suddenly came to a path. Looking to the left and the right and wondering whether to follow the easier route of the path, or continue through the undergrowth of the forest towards the street lamps, I suddenly heard a voice to my left. I quickly hid behind a tree and could feel my heart beating in my chest. I had decided a lot earlier that I was a definite coward, I now knew it to be a fact.

Glimpsing carefully around the tree, with my back to the lower part of the forest, I looked to the right. I could distinctly see a figure walking slowly up the path in my direction and that the person was carrying a large backpack from which curved upwards a large aerial. As the figure got closer, I saw that he had a headset over his beret was holding a microphone up to his mouth. I wondered whether to remain concealed and keep as quiet as possible, or to challenge him and find out which side he was on. What I should have done if he had been a part of the attacking force, I do not know.

I waited until he was almost on top of me and, plucking up courage I stepped out from behind the tree, shouting, 'Halt, who goes there?'. I have never seen anyone jump so much in my life, the guy nearly did a cartwheel. I was relieved to find out that he was not a part of the attacking force but a member of the Barnton Quarry contingent. After we had sorted out who was who, the radio operator contacted the control centre and made them aware of my position. My instructions were to make my way back as best as I could to the unit. I thanked my newly found friend and then proceeded down the path in the direction that he had come from, whilst he continued up the path in the opposite direction. After a while, the street lamps on my right seemed to be nearer and so I turned back into the forest making my way towards the road. I eventually came to a stone wall with rounded stone on the top and climbed over, dropping about five feet onto a narrow pavement. Using my geographical knowledge of the position of Barnton Quarry on the map, I knew that I was on the north side of the unit. I guessed that RAF Turnhouse would be off to the left of the road I had just joined. I turned left therefore and started walking along this road. I found out later that this was the Queensferry Road, which led to Queensferry, where the Forth railway bridge crossed the river. After some considerable time, and still carrying my Sten gun, I eventually found RAF Turnhouse and reported to the guardroom. The SP on duty must have been a bit of a softy, he told me to go to my hut, get some sleep and get some transport back up to Barnton Quarry the next day.

The next day after breakfast, I managed to get transport back to the Caledonian Sector Operations Centre and eventually met up again with my mates. Incredibly I had not been missed, which made me feel very wanted. I learned the news that the exercise was over and that Barnton Quarry had been wiped out. Not by our friends, the attacking RAF Regiment, who had incidentally breached the perimeter fence, by two men literally throwing one of their mates over the fence, but by a lone airman, a corporal technician, who had walked into the unit and got past the SPs at the police desk. Once in the block, he had planted dummy bombs at several vital places within the underground establishment. The strange thing was that, there wasn't a single corporal technician attached to the unit, or posted in from the other units on attachment to Barnton Quarry. So much for security!!.

Before we were returned to our own units, we were given a couple of days off to sample the fleshpots of Edinburgh. Actually, a gang of Longley Lane lads scrounged a lift into the city centre and was dropped opposite the Scott Monument on Princes Street. From there we split into small groups and went off to explore the city. My little party made our way up the Royal Mile to the Edinburgh Castle esplanade and into the castle. We did not have to pay to go in the castle, so, whether it was free for everyone at that time, or it was because we were in uniform, I do not know. I do know that we explored the castle for free.

Up on the battlements and beside the place from where the gun is fired over the city at one-o'clock each day, we stuck our heads through the castellated parts of the wall and looked down at the city's main railway station way below. Whilst I was looking out through one of the lowered sections of the wall, gazing at the railway lines, the activity in the station and on Princes Street, one of my so called mates grabbed me by the waist and did a quick forward and backward movement with my body, whilst hanging on to my belt. It took me by surprise and made me jump. Although I couldn't have fallen, because of the width of the wall, I was not pleased and called him something nice. Everybody else thought it was funny and laughed.

After an enjoyable visit to the castle we made our way back down the Royal Mile and through the winding streets back to Princes Street. We had a meal in a restaurant-cum snack bar and then wandered along Princes Street enjoying the brightly lit shop windows and eyeing up the local talent. At the far end of Princes Street, we came across a cinema. The film showing was 'East of Eden' with James Dean. A vote was taken and we all decided that a sit down in the cinema for a couple of hours would be a good way of resting our weary legs. I can't say that I enjoyed the film particularly, but the sit down was welcome. Now every time I see something to do with James Dean, my mind wanders back to that group of young airmen in the cinema in Edinburgh. After leaving the cinema, we wandered around trying to find how we could get back to RAF Turnhouse. Eventually a helpful bus inspector guided us in the right direction and we caught a bus back to the camp gates. We managed one more visit into the city before returning back to Preston and that was an evening visit. Again we wandered along Princes Street, popping into several pubs that we spotted up streets leading from the main street.

At one point we were walking along, having a laugh and the occasional joke, when we were alerted to some "brown jobs" (soldiers) on the other side of the road. They were obviously from one of the Scottish regiments, as they wore 'Tam-o-Shanters' and plaided trews. They were shouting something, but all we could make out was 'Brylcreem Boys', the rest of their shouts being in broad Scottish brogue, which we couldn't understand. They probably didn't understand the couple of lads who retaliated by shouting back, but we quickly shut up the two, as none of us wanted any trouble. We decided to ignore them and, after a couple more shouts, the soldiers went on their way.

Eventually we left the beautiful city of Edinburgh and returned to our own unit at Longley Lane.

On the first day back on duty, we all exchanged stories of our adventures 'abroad'. The lads who had been to Cyprus were noticeably sun-tanned and told of days spent on the beaches, whilst the ones who had been to Germany were full of stories about their conquests over the local German girls. Although we had enjoyed our sojourn to Scotland's capital city, most of us kept quiet, as we felt that the others who had travelled out of the country had a more adventurous time than we had.

Another time when we moved en-masse to another location, was when we were loaned out to RAF Hooton Park, near Birkenhead, for a 'Battle of Britain' open day, in September 1955.

Those of us chosen to go left the MT yard in one of the newer coaches. Corporal Skipper, the guy in charge of our MT section, drove the coach. We set off early from Warton, all of us looking extremely smart in our specially 'bulled' best blues. When we arrived at Hooton Park, the general public was all ready massing into the station. We drove into the station through a side entrance, to which a RAF policeman directed us, and on to one of the main hangars. We were to be used to demonstrate our plotting techniques to the unsuspecting world. Set up outside the hangar, in a roped off area, was a plotting table about half the size of our table at Longley Lane.

We donned headsets and plugged in to the dead plugs and plotted away, making up fictitious tracks. It was all right at first, but got very boring after a while, (except when there were young girls looking over the ropes, when we tended to show off somewhat). Every so often we were relieved by our colleagues and had the chance to wander around the static aircraft displays and the stalls, as well as having the opportunity see some real flying aircraft. Nearby our little roped off area, there was a large RAF van, which had steps leading into (at the front) and out of (at the back) the vehicle. Inside the van it was dark and there were a number of erks sitting in front of Radar screens. Members of the public were wandering through the van, looking at the equipment on display.

My mate and I spotted a lovely skive, helping people into and out of the van, which meant offering our hand to those members of the public requiring assistance, particularly young females, although there seemed to be more middle-aged and elderly women and men entering the vehicle.

During the flying display, three Vampires of (we found out later) 610 Squadron (County of Cheshire), flew across the airfield in a flying display. As they made about their third pass along the runway, from right to left, they moved from normal flight and each turned its port wings to face the ground in an aerobatic manoeuvre. Suddenly, in a flash, one of the aircraft dipped right down and literally flew straight into the ground. There was a massive explosion, the ground shook and clouds of black smoke rose into the air.

Most of the people didn't realise what had happened and seemed to think that the fire engines belting along the runway, in the direction of the downed plane were a part of the day's demonstrations. We found out afterwards that the pilot, killed in the crash, was a weekend pilot of the Auxiliary Air Force. Some of the aircraft I remember seeing at the open day were, Meteors, Hawker Hunters in the Black Arrows display team, American Sabre jets, a Lancaster bomber, some Lincoln bombers, Canberra bombers and many others. I saw more aircraft on that day than the rest of my time in the RAF.

As the show drew to a close, the general public slowly drifted away and the crowds thinned out. We were detailed to strip down the plotting table and to carry all the equipment we had been using into the hangar, in front of which our display had been set up. Eventually, after some tidying up, we boarded our coach and left Hooton Park for our journey back to Warton.

Most of us just sat looking out of the coach window, as our vehicle made its way out onto the roads outside the RAF station. There were still a few stragglers who had stayed at the show until the end and then hung back to avoid the traffic jams. Eventually our coach got out onto the East Lancs road. This highway was one of the forerunners of the modern motorways. It was a dual carriageway and had a special strip along the grass verge, which was reserved for cyclists. Traffic on the road was moderate and Skipper had the coach going at nearly full bore, about 55mph.

Suddenly, a coach full of females overtook us. The lads on the offside of our coach gave out a large cheer and those of us on the nearside, alerted to what was passing us, dashed across to the offside, leaning over our mates, shouting and waving, blowing kisses and generally making fools of ourselves.

The coach slowly pulled ahead of us and then moved into our lane in front of our vehicle. We all edged Skipper on and giving the coach all he had got, Skipper pulled into the right lane and started to pass the other coach, our coach was struggling, but slowly started to overtake the coach full of girls.

This time, my side of the coach had the prime viewing position and the lads on the offside, threw themselves across us, frantically waving to the girls on the other coach. This 'nip and tuck' situation went on until we met a gradient. The other coach driver must have been getting the same encouragement from his passengers, as he joined the overtaking game. Eventually as we hit the gradient, the civvie coach pulled away from us to our chagrin and disappeared up the road. No matter how much encouragement we gave to Skipper, he could get no more speed out of the coach and we thought that we had seen the last of our newly found female friends.

Further along the road, one of the keen-eyed erks at the front of the coach spotted the civvie vehicle in a pub car park where crowds of girls, in dirndl skirts and blouses (the fashion at that time) were milling around the car park. As we sped past, the lads from the offside dashed to the nearside once again. We were all shouting, cheering and waving frantically. The girls spotted us and waved back. One of the lads went to the sergeant and pleaded with him to stop the coach and go back to the pub. After some serious pressure from us all, Skipper went round the next island and headed back down the other carriageway. We had to pass the pub and carry on until we could go around the next island. As we passed the pub we could see that the car park was now empty apart from the civvie coach and a few cars.

Eventually we got back onto the eastbound carriageway and arrived at the public house about thirty minutes after we had last waved to the girls. Our sergeant said we could have just one drink but would then have to leave in order to get back to Warton at a reasonable hour.

You can imagine the situation when a coach-load of young airmen entered the pub, inhabited mainly by young women. We had a fabulous evening.

The girls were coupon checkers from the Littlewood's football pools firm and most of them were attractive and unattached (or so they said). As the night wore on, our sergeant was panicking and eventually ordered Skipper to phone Warton to make some excuse about engine problems with the coach.

The outcome was that we stayed until closing time and after we left the pub the car park was full of snogging airmen and coupon checkers. In the words of the Johnny Ray song, '*Ooh what a night it was, it really was such a night*'.

The couples were eventually prised apart and we reluctantly boarded our respective vehicles, sadly waving to our newly found 'girlfriends'. Some of the lads corresponded with the girls and incredibly one airmen eventually married one of the Littlewood's football pool coupon checkers.

I often wonder how their marriage went and of the incredible odds against meeting one's future wife in such a way. If our sergeant had been stricter and had refused to let Skipper turn the coach around, we would have never met the girls face to face and our colleague would have married someone else, probably from his own part of the country.

I can't remember what time we arrived back at Warton, but it was very late and certainly after midnight. We had had an extremely long and exciting day and we all went to bed contented and a little merry. I for one have never forgotten that special 'Battle of Britain' day.

10. Demob Time

(Where I become an 'old sweat')

By the time 1956 came around I felt I was a real 'old sweat'. I had been a Senior Aircraftman (SAC) for some considerable time and felt capable of doing most of the jobs that were done by ordinary 'erks' at Longley Lane. As mentioned previously, I had made life comfortable by the number of skives in which I was involved.

As the year progressed some of my mates finally reached the end of their service and achieved their ultimate aim in life at that time, which was to leave the service. I found myself attending more and more demob parties. Most Saturday nights were spent in Lytham or St. Annes or one of the local hostelries, celebrating someone's impending departure the following week. I never had too much to drink as some did, I never seemed to have enough spare cash. We had a 'demob fund', to which most of the senior airmen contributed, but we never seemed to accumulate enough money for more than one round of drinks.

One memorable night we all went into Lytham and spent a good evening of celebration, most of us making the last bus back to camp on time. When the bus started off, we were aware that two of our group was missing, we were not worried as we just thought that they would have a long walk back to 8 site. When they failed to report for morning parade, we were somewhat concerned, but then suspected that they may have reported sick with a hangover. Later that day, they turned up at the block somewhat shamefaced, they had spent the night as guests of the local constabulary and had appeared in the local magistrates court, where they were fined for being drunk and disorderly'. It appeared that when we were walking back to catch the bus, one of the miscreants had been taken short and decided to have a wee in a shop doorway. Whilst he was doing his dirty deed, his mate stood waiting quite innocently. Suddenly out of nowhere PC Plod arrived and promptly grabbed the airman who was watering the shop doorway. As he tried to march the guilty one off, his friend, who was somewhat inebriated, grabbed the policeman's arm saying, 'If you're taking him, you're taking me'. The policeman had replied by advising the silly airman to get on his way, in no uncertain terms. The drunken 'erk' insisted that, if his mate was being arrested then the policeman should arrest him too.

The arrested airman, who though guilty of urinating in a public place, was not as drunk as his mate, joined the policeman in telling the insistent 'erk' to go away. After our drunken friend said for the third time that he was not going to leave his mate to an unknown fate, the policeman lost his cool and granted him his wish, grabbing him by the collar and taking him to the local 'nick'. After a nights sleep in a cell, the two airmen appeared before the morning court, where the magistrate fined them for being drunk and disorderly. It did not finish there because their late arrival back at the unit saw them being charged with being absent without leave, for which they both received five days 'jankers'. It was some time before that pair became inebriated again.

Later that year we met some real 'old sweats' in the form of a group of 'Z' Reservists who spent their 15 days compulsory 'call to the colours', at our unit. They were a scruffy lot, who were somewhat unruly. They had done their National Service, but were called back as 'Z' Reservists for fifteen days of training. The ones that we met must have been some of the last 'Z' Reservists to be called up, when I left the service I never got called and was placed on 'H' reserve, so when the 15 days compulsory training situation changed I do not know.

The 'Z' men were billeted in the old Nissen huts, opposite from our huts and each day it was an education to see the way they paraded. They knew that not much could be done against them and so their discipline was nil. Whether they were typical of every 'Z' Reservists, or whether we just got an unruly bunch, I don't know.

In the early hours of one morning, I woke to the cry of 'Fire!'. I immediately jumped out of bed to see smoke coming from under the door that led into the small corridor at the entrance to the hut. By this time most of the other lads were out of bed. Thinking our main route of escape was blocked, we all started opening the hut windows and one by one we jumped out. When I landed on the grass, between the huts I became aware of the sound of laughing coming from the direction of the Nissen huts, it was our 'Z' Reservist friends, standing in a group and all having a good laugh at our expense.

What had happened was, that they had dragged a dustbin into the entrance corridor to our hut, set fire to the rubbish in the bin and put the lid back on. This had caused the fire proper to go out, but smoke was rising from the top of the bin. Presumably it was one of them who had shouted 'Fire!', in order to wake us up. They thought it was funny, we didn't. The next day we made a complaint to the CO, he said that, whilst he was concerned by the foolish actions of the 'Z' men, but there was little he could do about the situation.

Another occasion when our beauty sleep was disturbed was the direct result of an IRA raid on one of the armouries at RAF Warton. The time must have been about half-past three in the morning. We were all well in dreamland, when we were rudely awakened by a sergeant who was shouting to everyone to get out of bed. Apparently one of the armouries had been broken into and a number of weapons stolen. Once dressed we all paraded and were marched down to the site armoury, where we were issued with a .303 rifle, but no ammunition.

We all stood milling around, no one seemed to know what we were supposed to be doing. Eventually we were marched down to the MT yard and for some strange reason transported off to Longley Lane. What we were supposed to do with rifles with no bullets is debatable, especially as the rifles had been stolen from one of the sites at Warton and there was no weaponry that I was aware of stored at RAF Longley Lane. My mate Mick Dickinson, who was on 2 site at Warton, remembers the incident, as they were turned out on their site also. Whether the stolen rifles were ever recovered, we never found out, but it was put down to the IRA.

On the home front, my mates Tony Baxter and Mick Staniland, had both come to the end of their National Service. Tony had come back from abroad as a sun-tanned corporal, travelling back on the same troopship that took him to the Far East, the Empire Orwell. Tony had learned to drive in the army and on demob got a job as a van driver. Mick Stan had, following his accident, been shoved from pillar to post, the army seemingly not knowing what to do with him. He spent some considerable time at Richmond in North Yorkshire and then received a posting to Chester, which was fairly fortunate for him, as his married sister lived in that city.

A memorable thing happened to me about this time. I had a week's leave and went home. Knowing Tony was now home, I went to his house and we resumed our friendship, which had been interrupted by his being posted abroad. Tony told me of some of his adventures in Malaya. This country was on constant alert at that time, due to Communist terrorists who were murdering both British civilians and servicemen. When I consider some of the hardships suffered by National Servicemen in places like Malaya, Cyprus, Kenya and other places, I think I had quite a cushy time. After we had discussed our various service experiences, Tony told me of his interest in a girl, who he had seen whilst driving his delivery van.

He knew of her whereabouts in the evening and he suggested that we try and meet up with her and her friend. Well, to cut a long story short, we did eventually meet up with the girls, the one he fancied and her friend. I went along to make up a foursome. The upshot was that, the friend of the girl Tony was interested in, turned out to be Elsie, the girl who eventually became my wife. Tony's infatuation with Elsie's friend didn't last, but Elsie and I eventually became engaged and subsequently married after over two years courtship. After our initial meeting, we went to the cinema and saw a film titled 'The Man with the Golden Arm', about a man with a drugs problem and starring Frank Sinatra. At that time we were innocent of such things as drug taking and could not understand what the film was about.

The following day we spent in the Graves Park, a large park in Sheffield, and spent the rest of the week seeing one another. When I went back to camp, I couldn't wait for my next 36-hour pass. I now had a new interest in life. Although I was home most weeks, Elsie and I still corresponded, exchanging letters on a regular basis. I was now really looking forward to my demob.

About four months before my demob date was due, an offer was made to me and some of the other senior aircraftmen, to remuster. A new trade of Radar Observer (Aircrew) was open for volunteers from our trade. The sergeant advised us that, if we volunteered and passed the training course, we would immediately be promoted to the rank of sergeant. There were some volunteers, but I was now looking forward to leaving the service. We found out afterwards that the lads who had taken up on the offer, were posted to the Christmas Islands in the Pacific and were there when the Hydrogen Bombs were tested. Many years later, many of the servicemen who were present at the tests, developed cancer. It's amazing how people's lives can be changed by a decision made many years before.

Also in 1956, a crisis was building up in the Middle East. President Nasser of Egypt nationalized the Suez Canal and was subjected to all sorts of threats from Great Britain and France; the rest is history. He blocked the canal by sinking block-ships at the entrance and eventually Britain and France invaded. But that was later in the year. As the crisis built up, the government were calling back certain servicemen, who had only been demobbed a few months. Those of us who were nearing the end of our service, were fearing the worst. All sorts of rumours abounded. Our service was to be extended, some of us would be posted abroad, if a war started, we could be kept in the service indefinitely, it was all very worrying.

Two silly things happened to me during this period.

My sister Shirley, had been courting and had become engaged to an army friend of my brother Ken. Doug Partridge had been a regular in the Royal Signals and had met up with Ken in Germany. Doug hailed from Portsmouth and when on leave, he had accompanied my brother, staying at our house for a week. Doug and Shirley hit it off and continued to write to one another after his return to Germany. After Doug's demob they had arranged to get married in September 1956, which coincided with my release date. He was one of those who were recalled to their regiment as a result of the Suez crisis. When Doug found that he was going to be posted to Tripoli in North Africa, he applied for and was granted compassionate leave, in order that he and Shirley could get married by special licence. The vicar at Heeley Parish Church had said that he would allow them to bring their marriage date forward so that they could be married before Doug's overseas posting.

I knew nothing of these arrangements. We hadn't a telephone at home, so my father asked the owner of our corner shop, if he could telephone RAF Warton, to see if I could also have compassionate leave to attend the marriage. Mr Marsden the man from the corner shop, phoned Warton, who in turn put him through to RAF Longley Lane. This was on the Friday, as the rearranged wedding was supposed to take place on the Saturday.

Attached to our unit was an MT driver, SAC Boyce. When Mr Marsden asked the sergeant SP, to whom he was put through, if SAC Voyse could have a compassionate leave, the SP must have misheard him. He looked at the leave register and saw that SAC Boyce was scheduled to be on a 48 hour pass that weekend and told Mr Marsden, 'He'll not need compassionate leave, he's on his way home this weekend on a 48 hour pass'. Mr Marsden passed on that message to my dad. Normally, when I left Longley Lane at the end of my shift, I could be home in less than four hours. When I had not arrived home by midnight, my parents were in a bit of a panic, wondering what had happened to me. I of course was not on leave and spent the evening back at Warton oblivious to the events which were unfolding.

The next day, at about 10 o'clock, I was summoned to the police desk with the message that the Sheffield City Police wanted me on the phone. It was my turn to panic. With a thumping heart, wondering what had happened, I went to the police desk and was handed the phone by the duty policeman. The next bit sounds like something out of a Brian Rix farce. The telephone conversation went something like this:

Me: '*Hello*'

Policeman at the other end of the line: '*Is this SAC Voyse?*'

Me: '*Yes*'.

I could hardly get my words out because of the panic I was in.

Policeman: '*Why haven't you come home?*'

Me (puzzled): '*I'm not supposed to be coming home. What's happened?*'

Policeman: '*I've had a Mr Marsden on the phone. You're supposed to be marrying his daughter today.*'

Me (totally puzzled): '*I only know one Mr Marsden and his daughter is only a baby*'.

Policeman: '*Are you sure?*'

Me (still puzzled): '*Yes, of course I'm sure! I've got a girlfriend, but we have not planned to get married. The only wedding I know about is my sister's and that is not until September.*'

Policeman: '*I'll have to make further enquiries and get back to you*'.

Me (extremely puzzled) '*O.K...*'

End of conversation!

Later that day I received a message that it was my sister who was getting married that day, by which time it was far too late for me to do anything about attending the wedding. On my sister's wedding photographs, Elsie can be seen, but I am noticeable by my absence. Doug and Shirley eventually emigrated to Australia, with their one and only offspring Colin, but, as they say, that's another story.

On one of the weekends shortly after that event, I was on leave when I received a telegram to report back to Longley Lane immediately and; once again panic set in. At Sheffield Victoria station, I met a number of the other lads who had received similar telegrams. All sorts of suggestions abounded as to why we had been summoned back. On arrival at Preston, we caught the

'Ribble' bus service destined for Garstang. The bus travelled out of Preston along the A6 until it reached Barton crossroads. At that point it turned right. We were on the upper deck of the bus and as it approached the crossroads, we were perturbed to see a military policeman, complete with red topped cap, white webbing and white gauntlet type gloves, on point duty at the Barton crossroads junction. The MP had his back to us and his right hand was extended, his left hand was waving to the drivers of sand coloured Bedford trucks, with canvas backs, which were coming from the opposite direction to us and were turning left into Whittingham Lane.

We all looked at one another in PANIC! Eventually there was a break in the convoy of trucks and the MP waved our bus right into Whittingham Lane. Our fears were somewhat allayed, when we saw that the trucks were being waved right, into a Royal Army Service Corps depot, which was situated on Whittingham Lane. We found out later that they were being delivered from a storage centre in Carlisle and were being refuelled at the RASC depot.

When we arrived at Longley Lane, we found that we had been called back to deal with the extra amount of air traffic, created by aircraft on training flights and practice interceptions, in preparation for the events which developed later in the Middle East. We were all relieved to find that we were not destined to go to the same destinations to which the sand-coloured trucks were headed.

The time for my nearing demob, coincided with the worsening events in the Middle East. Rumours abounded, those of us due for demobilization were fearful of having our service extended. Every night we were glued to the television in the NAAFI, watching the nightly news, and the Prime Minister, Anthony Eden, addressed the nation. At that time I always thought that whatever Britain did was right and was for the good of others. Looking back in hindsight I now realize that other people had rights and that the use of 'bully boy' tactics was wrong.

Contrary to my fears I was not obliged to stay in the Air Force when my demob time came. I can't remember much about my own demob party, but I'm sure that my friend Chris and me must have had an evening out with the lads. I went around my friends shaking hands and promising to keep in touch. Regrettably a lot of the promises which were made from both sides were not kept and so contact was lost with the people who had been my constant companions during my time at Warton and Longley Lane. The CO granted us a short visit to his office, where he shook hands with me and Chris and wished us all the best for the future. In the Administration office, my friend Ted gave me my release documents, which carried a résumé of my service. Ted told me that the documents bore a forgery of the CO's signature, as it was rare for him to sign the release documents, and it was inevitably a member of the Admin Staff who signed the document.

The day came around when, instead of joining the rest of the lads on the transport up to the block, I stayed behind and packed up my kit. I stripped my bed for the last time and stowed the sheets and pillow cases away in the laundry room. The blankets on my bed were folded and placed at the head of the bed and, after a long look around I left hut 148 and joining Chris headed for the main gate. At the guardroom, the SP checked our final leave passes and we walked out of the camp to freedom and stood at the bus stop waiting for the 'Ribble' bus for Preston. Being in uniform, it still did not feel that I had left the RAF, there had been no trumpets blowing or banners waving as we left the service, we simply walked out of the main gate and out of the service of the Royal Air Force.

The following week, I re-joined my old employer and became a real 'old sweat', regaling my stories of life in the Royal Air Force, at any opportunity I was given.

'Per Ardua Ad Astra'
or, as we used to say,
'Nil Desperandum Carborundum'
('Don't let the bastards grind you down')

11. Postscript

Prior to going into the Royal Air Force, I was dreading doing my National Service. I had heard all sorts of tales from people who had been in the services or who had been called up and done their square-bashing. Looking back on the experience after many years, I realised that the two years I spent away from home, had done me a lot of good. There was the companionship of other young men who were in the same predicament, people who would fall over themselves to help you, as they had been helped by others. There were times when I had the pants scared off me and there were times when things were so funny I nearly cried. I saw places in the country that I might not have seen had I not done National Service.

Things were so different in the 'Fifties'. Very few people went abroad for their holidays, most people, (if they were fortunate) had a week at the seaside. Pleasures were simple, nearly every night I went to the cinema with my friends. We did have a television at home but those that were available were black and white, with a twelve-inch screen and only one channel. The television service started late every evening and finished early. At our house we were avid radio listeners. 'Dick Barton – Special Agent' was a must every night at 6.45pm. When the nightly news came on, we all had to be quiet whilst Dad listened to the world events. I did a lot of reading, I visited the library every week.

After leaving the service I went back into the grocery and provisions trade for a year and then, seeking more pay, joined the Sheffield Transport Department as a Bus Conductor. I stayed with the firm for nearly thirty years, leaving the successor company South Yorkshire Passenger Transport Executive in the rank of Chief Traffic Officer in 1986. That however is another story.

I lost touch with my old RAF mates, although on the odd occasion I would bump into one of the several lads who lived in Sheffield. In 1995, I made contact with a few of those who had been based at the Western Sector CFP (Centralized Filter Plotting) unit Whittingham Lane and every two years since I have been to a reunion. I have never been able to locate my special mate Ted who hailed from Bolton. We communicated for about two years, then either one or the other of us stopped writing. During the early part of my career on the buses I was working long hours and so I always seemed to be tired when I got home from work. I was never in the mood for letter writing after a long shift at work.

In 1992 whilst on holiday in the Lake District, I came across a display stand for the Royal Observer Corps, which was at a show in Bowness on Lake Windermere. I picked up one of the leaflets and lo and behold there was the address of my former unit, although the leaflet showed 'Langley' Lane, rather than 'Longley' Lane. The rest of the address was Goosnargh near Preston so I knew it must be our unit. A couple of years later, we booked to stay at a caravan site in Clitheroe, Lancashire, so, prior to going away, I rang the telephone number on the leaflet and was able to speak to the Commanding Officer of the ROC unit. I explained who I was and asked if it would be possible to visit Longley Lane, whilst we were staying in Lancashire. At that time I was a serving Special Constable and mentioned that fact also. The CO told me to give him a call, once we were at the caravan site at Clitheroe and he would arrange something. On Monday, following our arrival at the caravan site the previous Saturday, I rang the unit again. The upshot was that not only was I invited to visit the site, but I was given the permission for my wife Elsie, my friend Mick Dickinson and his wife, Carole, to visit the unit. So Elsie got the opportunity to visit the underground bunker I had spoken about for years.

The CO himself gave us a guided tour. The structure itself had changed very little, there's very little you can do with ten feet thick concrete walls, the Operations room was quite different, the function of the unit was to monitor nuclear strikes on the United Kingdom. Fire doors had been fitted half way along the underground corridors and at the end of the unit, behind what had been the 'fixers', an extension to the bunker had been constructed. This contained additional equipment that was designed to allow the unit to operate for up to 30 days after any nuclear strike.

Outside the block, on what had been the vehicle park in my day there, a series of pre-fabricated buildings had been erected which were being used as the Administrative Offices of the ROC.

Not long after our visit, the Royal Observer Corps ceased to exist and all the units throughout the UK from which it had operated, including Longley Lane, were closed down .

In the year 2000 I was obliged to visit Blackpool on business. Looking at the road map, I saw that Junction 1 of the M55 was about a mile from the Barton crossroads. I decided to have a look at the bunker to see what had happened since its second occupier had left. I was accompanied by my young second in command from work, a girl who, incredibly, had been brought up in Freckleton (her parents still live there).

The surface buildings, described above, are now the offices of a Veterinary Surgeon. The doors to the bunker, both at the side and at the back, where the extension had been built, were wide open. I couldn't get close to the main doors, by which we used to enter the bunker, because of a barbed wire fence. The back doorway was full of hay, which I suppose was the fodder for the horses we spotted in a surface building which was now a stable. I took a number of photographs.

From Longley Lane we drove through Goosnargh village and down Whittingham Lane. The gates on the perimeter fence around the old CFP were securely locked and on the grass verge, at the side of the fence was a sign, 'FOR SALE – FORMER MINISTRY OF DEFENCE BUNKER'.

Once again I used my camera. Leaving the former CFP, which I understand, had been used by the army, following the RAF's departure, I went on the search for the former QQ site (of Eric the ghost fame). I went down a private farm road, which ran alongside the M6 motorway, until I reached a farmyard, which had a gate, which was closed. I never found QQ, so, whether it is buried under the motorway, or it was down the other side, from where I was searching, I don't know.

Later on in the year, whilst searching on the computer through the 'Internet' sites with my son, on the computer, we came across a site titled 'Subterranea Britannica'. I couldn't believe it. There on the site was a description of Longley Lane, along with photographs and an interior shot. Not only that, but a photograph of a well vandalised Barnton Quarry (the Caledonian Sector Operations Centre) was also shown on the site, the underground unit having suffered a worse fate than Longley Lane, due to a serious fire affecting the bunker. It was found that a great deal of 'Blue Asbestos' had been used in the construction of the site and the complete unit had been permanently sealed.

And so ends my story. I suppose that everyone has a period in their life which is something special, for me the 'Fifties' were extra special. I went into the 'Fifties' as an innocent thirteen-year-old boy, and by the end of the decade, I was a young married man with a baby daughter.

Additional Photographs

RAF Cardington. The author is extreme left, back row. Friend Chris, who stayed with me throughout service, is third from the right in the back row, with tilted hat.

The main gate at RAF West Kirby, Wirral. (© RAF Museum)

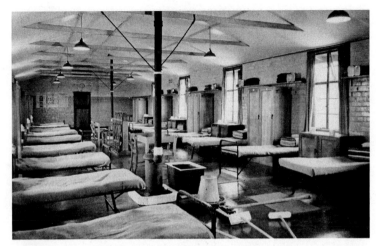

Typical RAF Nissen Hut interior at West Kirby.

Our friends the drill instructors (note weighted trousers of the DI on the right).

Group with berets like flying saucers in most cases. Mick (the painter and signwriter) is second from left in the front row (with bandaged carbuncle). The author is standing third from right in the back row.

Group of 'trained killers' with sergeant and corporal drill instructors. The author is second from left in the front row, dangerously armed with a Lee Enfield 303 rifle; beret now under control.

The author and Mick Staniland after his recovery from serious injury, taken in Meersbook Park, Sheffield.

The two Micks — Staniland and Dickinson.

A group of plotters at RAF Warton with 'haunted' Nissen huts in the background.